WITH VERBAL JUDO, YOU'LL LEARN HOW TO:

Look at conflict creatively

Remain under emotional control during disagreements

Find solutions to potentially difficult situations

Maintain professionalism in any context

Use words instead of actions to achieve goals

Avoid using language that expresses personal feelings
during conflicts

Employ empathy to stay engaged with people while
maintaining self-control

Use words that are on target by first understanding the
listener's point of view

Ensure that you are understood

Achieve cooperation and break through uncertainty,
confusion, anger, mistrust, and even prejudice

Communicate with difficult people without shaming,
blaming, or manipulating

Safely take action when words fail

About the Author

GEORGE J. THOMPSON (aka Doc Rhino) is the president and founder of the Verbal Judo Institute, a police training and management consultant firm now based in Yucca Valley, California. He has taught English at the high school and university levels, worked as a police officer, and holds black belts in both judo and Tae Kwon Do. He has applied his diverse experience and background by developing the only nationally recognized course in tactical communication, Verbal Judo. Recently, Doc Rhino has created courses specially designed for educators and medical and airline personnel who frequently have to deal with difficult and often violent people. He has taught more than 175,000 police officers, and his Verbal Judo course is required police training in numerous states across the country. Doc Rhino received his B.A. from Colgate University, his masters and doctorate in English from the University of Connecticut, and completed postdoctoral work at Princeton University in rhetoric and persuasion. He is widely published in magazines and national periodicals, and his training has appeared on such national networks and shows as NBC, ABC, LETN, *CBS News, CNN, 48 Hours, Inside Edition, In the Line of Duty,* and *Fox News.* Doc and his wife, Pam, recently had a baby boy, Tommy Rhyno Thompson. You can contact Doc Rhino personally at woosha @aol.com or at his office e-mail, verbaljudo@rmi.net, or write to P.O. Box 2263, Yucca Valley, CA 92286. Enjoy his website at www.verbaljudo.com.

VERBAL JUDO

The Gentle Art of Persuasion

George J. Thompson, Ph.D.,
and
Jerry B. Jenkins

Quill
An Imprint of HarperCollinsPublishers

Published in association with the literary agency of Alive Communications, P.O. Box 49068, Colorado Springs, Colorado 80949.

HarperCollins books may be purchased for educational, business, or sales promotional use. For information please write: Special Markets Department, Harper-Collins Publishers Inc., 10 East 53rd Street, New York, NY 10022.

First Quill edition published 1994.

Library of Congress Cataloging-in-Publication Data is available.

ISBN 0-06-057765-7

08 09 RRD 20 19 18

To all who, like me, could have used this training twenty
years ago to help end the number one form of abuse in society—
verbal abuse

With a heartfelt salute to the street cops of America
who have shared their skills with me

And with thanks to my family,
who might have wished I had been a quicker learner

CONTENTS

A DECADE LATER

THIS LITTLE VOLUME you are holding in your hands, *Verbal Judo: The Gentle Art of Persuasion*, battled to survive when it was first launched into the crowded book marketplace in 1993. But little by little, readers began to embrace its hope-filled message of better relationships and better communication through empathy. Our seminars and training sessions began to swell with more and more enthusiastic participants and word spread that this Verbal Judo stuff really works!

We know of the book's impact from the hundreds of letters and e-mails we have received over the past decade. We know of its power from the many testimonials from our seminar participants, many of whom have come to the course more than once. As one put it last year, "You know, Doc, Verbal Judo changed my life, but I need to hear its gospel every two years or so." Another wrote me, shortly after attending a training session, "Thanks for saving my relationship with my teenage son. When I got home, I sat down and talked to my son, really for the first time in years. Verbal Judo turned me around. Thank you!" And then there was the police officer who attended my five-day instructor course. On day one, a Monday, he informed me, "I'm getting a divorce next week." By Thursday night he called me at my hotel to tell me, "You know, Doc, this course has hit home. I called my wife just now and told her we are putting off the divorce and heading to counseling, something she had wanted and I hadn't. I have learned I'm the problem, and I value my wife and kids and intend to make the necessary changes." A year later I got a Christmas card from him and his wife—happily together!

Such responses make me more committed than ever to sharing the powerful techniques in this book so they can benefit as many people as possible. During this past decade, I have personally trained thousands of police officers in hundreds of departments, ranging from LAPD and San Diego to Chicago, NYPD, and Miami Dade County, to mention only a few. Verbal

Judo is now required police training in most states, and the officers who use it are safer and more professional.

But Verbal Judo is more than just good training for police and other emergency personnel; it's useful for anyone. Years ago I modified it for the business and corporate world, and now my staff routinely teaches service professionals, airline personnel, state and federal employees, realtors, and anyone who works in the potentially "hot arena" of public service, sales, or business. Schoolteachers and administrators can greatly benefit from this training, as could doctors and medical staffs across the country. Even our kids need this training, which is why I'm developing a course specifically for them.

To further illustrate the need for Verbal Judo, I would like to share a personal experience. I recently underwent throat surgery for cancer. I lost my left vocal chord, and with it my ability to speak professionally, but I am now cancer free. I spent fifteen days in the hospital, frail and weak from the surgery, watched over by perhaps twenty or so nurses, doctors, and students. I couldn't sleep, I couldn't eat, and I could barely move. The quality of care was terribly uneven, ranging from awful to acceptable, with only one excellent. Nowhere was the need for Verbal Judo training more evident. Hardly anyone seemed to have any empathy for those of us who were hurt and scared—we were just "beds." Cold and impersonal was the norm; just a little human contact or a kind word would have made such a difference. And that difference is exactly what this book has to offer.

The entire basis of Verbal Judo is to treat people with dignity and respect, most of all your family and close friends. Be ever so careful how you speak to them, as words can cut deeper and fester longer than sword wounds. Ironically, we often spend less energy being kind to those closest to us. Change it! I learned again in the hospital what I've always striven to teach and know myself: In this life, the most important thing you have is your relationships with people. Verbal Judo can help you maintain those relationships and improve the quality of your life and the lives of those around you. It has saved lives, marriages, and careers—and it can work for you too. Use it!

INTRODUCTION

Communication as a Noncontact Sport

THE LAST THING Dr. George J. Thompson wants is for *Verbal Judo* to be merely an entertaining collection of true-life cop stories. Admittedly, it has its share of back-alley fights suddenly neutralized with left-field offers, suicide attempts derailed by wily candor, and domestic squabbles defused by a cop who knows how to intrude and do nothing. But *Verbal Judo* is much more.

A former college English literature professor, George Thompson is a black belt in both judo and tae kwon do karate, a combination that made one unusual police officer when he first put on a badge at age thirty-five.

Today, through his Verbal Judo Institute, he primarily trains cops how to use their mouths instead of their nightsticks and guns. He is also in demand by schoolteachers, hospital administrators, salespeople, and business executives. He has trained people at organizations ranging from IBM to the FBI, and from the U.S. Forest Service to Metropolitan Life. It is cops on the street, though, whose lives hang in the balance if they don't use language properly.

Among George Thompson's students have been six

thousand five hundred members of the Los Angeles Police Department. In fact, the four officers videotaped in the Rodney King incident were one week away from taking his Verbal Judo class. George Thompson believes that violence could have been avoided had the officers spent a day in his classroom.

In training tens of thousands of officers throughout the United States, George Thompson has developed foundational, state-of-the-art communication skills that are easy to learn and will work for anybody. He believes that Verbal Judo principles can save ordinary citizens unnecessary conflict, tension, and abuse. This book is intended for anyone who wants to reduce stress by using the most effective and powerful communication techniques available today. It is for people who like to get what they want by using responsible means—whether convincing a contractor that they have been overcharged or getting a boss to stop sexual harassment. *Verbal Judo* also effectively teaches parents how to motivate their children to do better in school—or how to protect themselves on the street.

Verbal Judo is designed for people who want more open and satisfying relationships—with their families, their colleagues, their employees, and their friends. Its techniques for establishing rapport and empathy can also help people enjoy improved relationships with the opposite sex. It is not uncommon for students to approach George Thompson after a class and ask, "Where were you two marriages ago?"

Verbal Judo is a manual for those who want a powerful communication breakthrough that can improve their lives.

What differentiates *Verbal Judo* from other books on communication is that it offers solutions that work when people are under pressure. It provides techniques that have been tested on the street by men and women responding in life-or-death situations.

Verbal Judo can develop in you habits of thinking and acting that George Thompson developed in his extensive study of the martial arts. It blends the best of an Eastern-style mind-set (particularly the notion of using the energy of negative situations) with such Western philosophies as the Golden Rule and even Aristotelian rhetoric, which Dr. Thompson studied in post-graduate work at Princeton.

Verbal Judo will teach you to respond—not react—to situations. Using what George Thompson calls "the most dangerous weapon on the street today: the cocked tongue," you will learn to adapt and be flexible, just as practitioners of physical judo do. You will learn to use your words to redirect the negative force of others toward positive outcomes.

You don't have to understand complex philosophies to become proficient in Verbal Judo. George Thompson teaches by simple example, through his own real-life experiences. He tells how he and other "salty old police dogs" cleverly talked their way out of danger. And he provides amusing anecdotes from his years as a parent, trying to outwit two gifted children.

In V*erbal Judo* you'll learn to speak with anybody without causing or escalating conflict. You'll learn to praise without sounding manipulative. And you'll learn to criticize so people remember what was said, are motivated to change, and still feel like valued team members. *Verbal Judo* also has solutions for dealing with people under the influence of liquor, drugs, fear, rage—or plain stupidity.

With George Thompson's tactics for mind-mouth harmony, you will learn far more than how to throw words around to live more safely in a treacherous world. You will learn a new habit of mind, a gentle approach taking control of situations without creating stress, without frustration, and without conflict.

As he clarifies in Chapter 17, "Nowhere did I learn these principles more clearly than on the streets as a cop. I use a lot of police examples, because I believe it is easy to transfer the principles to everyday civilian situations. My hope is that people might see police anecdotes as the essence of Verbal Judo in stark clarity. In other words, if it doesn't work on the street, you can't use it in the home or at the office. And if it does work on the street, well, see for yourself . . ."

1

Birth of a Communication Samurai

IT WAS THE most outrageous way to bust up a fight I had ever seen. I'd been a rookie cop ten days when my partner got the call. At two A.M. we were dispatched to break up a nasty domestic dispute in a tenement on the east side of Emporia, Kansas, notorious for drug dealing and random violence.

We could hear the couple's vicious, mouth-to-mouth combat from the street. My training sergeant and partner, Bruce Fair, and I approached and peeked through the half-open door. Then Bruce just walked in without bothering to knock. I watched as he strode right past the warring couple, took off his uniform cap, sighed, and planted himself on the couch. Ignoring the argument, he picked up a newspaper and thumbed through the classifieds!

Leaning against the door with my hand on the butt of my .357, I was flabbergasted. Bruce seemed to violate all the rules of police procedure. I had never seen him enter a house without identifying himself, without asking permission, or without at least saying why he was there. There he was, treating an angry couple in a tenement apartment as if he were a visiting uncle.

Bruce kept reading and the couple kept arguing, occasionally glancing at the cop on their couch. They had yet to notice me. As the man cursed his wife, Bruce rattled the newspaper. "Folks. Folks! Excuse me! Over here!"

The stunned husband flashed a double take. "What are you doing here?"

Bruce said, "You got a phone? Look here. A 1950 Dodge! Cherry condition! Can I borrow your phone? I know it's late, but I don't want to miss out on this. Where's your phone? I need to call right now!"

The husband pointed to the phone, incredulous. Bruce rose and dialed, then mumbled into the phone. He slammed it down. "Can you believe they wouldn't talk to me just because it's two in the morning?"

By now the fight had evaporated, the couple standing there as dumbfounded as I was. "By the way," Bruce said pleasantly, as if just becoming aware, "is anything the matter here? Anything my partner and I can do for you?"

The husband and wife looked at the floor and shook their heads. "Not really, no." We chatted with them a bit, reminding them that it was late and that everyone around would appreciate a little peace and quiet. Soon we were on our way.

Then I was really puzzled. Earlier that night we had broken up a similar dispute in the classic cop fashion. We quickly took control with polite authority, performed what's known as a "separate and suture" (where the warring parties are separated, calmed, and then brought back together), and diffused the situation. That was the way I had been trained, so what was this new twist?

I mean, as a former college English professor who had taught Milton and Shakespeare for ten years, I'd seen some ingenious twists of plot. But a cop taming two animals by intruding as a rude but friendly guest? Bruce had forced those people to play host to him whether or not they wanted to.

As soon as we were back in the squad car I asked him,

"What in the world was that all about? Why did we separate and suture earlier and pull this crazy newspaper-and-telephone gag just now?"

He shrugged. "I don't know. I've been on the street more'n ten years. You just learn."

"Hey, I may be new at this," I said, "but I'm no kid. [I was thirty-five.] I haven't got ten years. I could get blown away if I tried that stunt. We need to talk. Tell me how you knew you could get away with that."

I didn't realize it then, but that evening marked the birth of Verbal Judo and was the first lesson in my career as a communication samurai. I had studied the martial arts, starting with genuine Indian wrestling, since I was six and held black belts in judo and tae kwon do karate, but I had never seen such principles so effectively applied to life on the streets.

It was one thing to practice the martial arts in a storefront dojo with polite, honorable opponents bowing and working together, competing and learning. (In judo I had learned the gentle art of redirecting my opponent's energy to achieve my own goal. If he came straight at me, I would sidestep and try a move that would add to his momentum, carrying him past me where I could take control.) But I had watched Bruce Fair do virtually the same thing without an ounce of physical force. With his mouth, a newspaper, and a telephone, he had calmed two hotheads with redirective techniques he had absorbed through experience.

I was intrigued. During the remainder of my tenure as a police officer—working everything from canine patrol to hostage negotiations—I carefully watched and listened to guys like Bruce. I began systematically studying the communication techniques of salty old police dogs, carrying a tape recorder with me on every call. I listened not only to what was said, but also to *how* it was said. Time after time I saw older, street-savvy officers assume roles and counter-roles, suavely manipulating people's energies to calm otherwise dangerous situations.

I quickly became convinced that good police officers are the greatest communicators in the world. They often have to issue orders and elicit compliance from hostile subjects, as when they're derailing a drug deal and the gang members are reaching for their AK-47s. Despite my classical education, which had exposed me to the finest rhetoricians of the ages, I realized that my real postdoctoral work hadn't been done at Princeton. It was unfolding for me right on the streets of Emporia.

I've made every mistake you can make in communication, so I'm no guru addressing you from a state of perfection. Rather, I'm someone who's finally learned from his mistakes. If I can save you the kind of hassle I've endured, I'll consider this endeavor a success.

I have three overarching goals. First and most important is to ensure your personal safety. Developing mind-mouth harmony is the greatest skill in the world, because if you make a mistake with either you can find yourself in serious personal danger. You can lose a marriage, stall a career, instigate violence, lose your credibility, alienate people, and lose friends. I know, I've done them all.

Whether you are an executive or a homemaker, Verbal Judo, if for nothing else, is designed to keep you alive. Admittedly, police officers—the primary audience for my course over the years—are much more vulnerable to violence than the rest of us. In the last ten years 855 police officers were killed in the line of duty, and more than seven hundred times that number wound up in emergency rooms across the country. We know from research that almost all of those injuries began with mind-mouth disharmony. That's why I tell cops that the most dangerous weapon they carry is not the 9 mm or the .357 or the pump shotgun. Their most dangerous weapon is the cocked tongue. (More on that later.)

Goal number two is to enhance your professionalism. Regardless whether you're in retail, wholesale, on a police force, part of corporate America, or working at home, you're a professional. Everything I offer here can measurably improve your performance by reducing complaints from those you work with and reducing your personal stress.

If you can learn to use your words without causing strife and conflict, you will have fewer complaints in the work world and fewer arguments with your friends and family. This will go a long way in reducing stress, which is something you usually bring on yourself by the way you deal with people. Reduce your capacity for conflict, and you will reduce stress.

My third goal is to increase your efficiency by improving your performance level. This will have the added benefit of improving your self-esteem, the way you view yourself. Increasing your efficiency also means improving your ability to "say it right" the first time, rather than as so many of us do, having to apologize, restate, and try to explain why you fired off words that caused you problems in the first place.

If there was one thing I didn't like about my academic colleagues it was that too few of them could practically apply what they taught. You can imagine what they thought of me, this strange guy who liked to ride along with cops and play at judo and karate on the side!

I might have felt like a fish out of water in both the academic and the law enforcement worlds if I hadn't come up with the communication system that ties them together.

2

Motivating the Disagreeable

So YOU'LL SEE that I'm trying to teach you with your own best benefit in mind, let me tell you briefly what I've come to realize over the years about teaching. Teaching is the process of moving people from what they know to what they don't know. And I've found the best way to teach a motivated student is to appeal to his consciousness with a very small element of language, a metaphor and a simile, which is understandable to him so he can understand what is being taught.

A dry, boring teacher talks about what he knows, as if the student should have a clue. The student makes no movement. He hears the teacher talking about something the teacher may know well, but unless that teacher compares it to something within the range of that student's experience, little learning takes place.

At the other end of the spectrum—and also unacceptable—is the teacher who moves students from what they know to other areas they already also know.

I'd always been taught that a teacher masters his material, goes into the classroom, and presents it. The teacher presents, the student receives. If the student doesn't get it, he fails. But that's not the way the real world works. In the real world a teacher has to know his audience and start where they are, taking them to where they haven't been.

When you use Verbal Judo, you have an audience; you have someone on whom you practice Verbal Judo. Your audience may not be a class full of kids but an office full of employees. Maybe you're dealing with an audience of one: your boss or your spouse. Maybe it's a difficult child or a tough landlord or a problem neighbor. Regardless, like the cop on the street, you have to read your audience, know your principles—the tools with which to accomplish what you want in the situation—then decide which of the many methods will make your principles effect the outcome you want. Often the best way of reading your target audience is to see the person the way he sees himself. Which is the true essence of empathy.

Then, using the language of your audience, you can make the strange become familiar. Albert Einstein was brilliant at that. He would sit in Princeton Square and use balloons and oranges to explain the most complicated ideas. Carl Sagan does much the same. Great, profound thinkers must communicate simply. They understand the complexities, but they must make them simple so everyone can understand.

For example, you'll see case histories here where a cop is trying to calm a frightened, potentially violent troublemaker. In the classic macho approach, the cop would challenge the guy: "Put that knife down or I'll take you out! You haven't got a chance. I'll blow your head off," things like that. That virtually forces the man to attack, to defend his manhood, to save face.

But what if that cop gently empathizes and says, "Hey, friend, let's do each other a favor. You don't want to spend the night downtown with us, eating our food, sleeping on our steel cot, and missing your woman. And I don't want to sit at a typewriter for a couple of hours doing paperwork on this. If we can work this out, you can have dinner at your own table, be with your woman, and wake up in your own bed tomorrow morning. And I can go back about my business."

You'll come to see how this works, how the perpetrator becomes an ally with the officer to the benefit of both. What has happened? The officer has motivated a disagreeable person to a point of Voluntary Compliance—the ultimate goal of Verbal Judo. If you can see how learning that skill would improve your relationships and your life, you're a motivated student who has picked up the right book.

3

Baptism of Fire

MY BACKGROUND IS the strangest mix of the physical and the cerebral that I'm aware of. I'm a middle-aged jock with a chip on his shoulder who could just as easily scream in your face and wrestle you to the floor as smile and calm the situation with a well-chosen word. Don't I sound like an English Ph.D.?

I'm just like you. If I get cut off in traffic, my first impulse is revenge. If someone barks at me, my first reaction is to take his head off. Problem is, like most sane people, I'd regret it. It took me a while to realize that an expert on the art of Verbal Judo should be a man who needs it. Yeah, I do. It makes me chuckle to realize how quickly I can shake a fist (or a digit) at another driver while on my way to the airport to fly somewhere and teach my course on proper responses to negative situations.

I still say that makes me the right guy for the job. The success of my Verbal Judo Institute allows me to look back with gratitude—and not regret—on an upbringing that might have made another guy bitter.

I was the product of a soldier and his wife whose mar

riage soured before I turned three. My mother gave a porter a few dollars and asked him to watch out for me on a California-to-New York train ride to my grandparents in Ithaca, New York.

I recall growing up pretty much alone, walking the ravines as a mountain boy. One of the most significant things that happened to me was hooking up with an old Cherokee who taught me to trail and track. I. D. Swiftwater felt he owed my grandfather a debt of gratitude because my grandfather (a Cornell University law professor) while a student years before had done some *pro bono* legal work for him and kept him from losing his forty acres. So, Swiftwater took me under his wing and I enjoyed the rare privilege of learning Indian ways.

While being raised in the home of an Ivy League educator, where I read widely everyday and learned to speak correctly, I was one bitter kid. I had no idea I was getting a most unusually well-rounded background, with my grandparents' emphasis on schooling, the genteel world of higher education, and my inclination toward athletics. I felt rejected by my mother and a burden to my grandparents. From nursery school on, my records paint a picture of the real George Thompson, the child I recognize inside me today: with a hot temper and short fuse, has trouble getting along with others, etc., etc., etc.

Two philosophies warred within me: Take no crap from anyone, and look out for number one.

I hated school. I was always challenging, always asking why, never doing what I was told before demanding a reason. I wanted to win all arguments, all fights, all games. My record was full of dire predictions. In high school I was a star athlete, an all-American swimmer, but still I had never applied myself to my studies.

In the fall of 1959, as I began my senior year, a counselor took me aside, an old woman who had tried everything to get through to me. She said, "You may be some hotshot swimmer, but you're going to be a benchsitter in life. No college is going to accept somebody with your grades, and you're never going to amount to anything."

I sat there sullenly waiting for the lecture, the remedy, the typical "so you had better start applying yourself, young man" routine. But it never came. That was it. She was finished. She had pronounced judgment on me. They had tried everything to get through to me. I was worthless and wouldn't amount to anything, so best of luck.

She's probably long dead now, so I'll never find out, but to this day I don't know if she was cunning enough to know that challenging me like that was my only hope. I stormed out of there determined to show her.

And I did.

I became a straight A student overnight and was accepted at several prestigious colleges. I chose Colgate, where I majored in English. I still had an attitude, but I was learning to channel my anger and aggressiveness into more socially acceptable pursuits. I enjoyed reading and learning, thinking, analyzing, and discussing. Upon graduation, I wanted to teach. When a position opened at Princeton (New Jersey) High School, I went for it. I had no idea what I was getting into or how it would help shape my life.

I was to teach English and reading, including one remedial class. No one told me that the previous teacher had been beaten up and left bleeding in his car. I didn't learn till later that a woman teacher the year before had been dangled by her ankles from the second-floor window. This was a class that chewed up teachers and spit them out.

"Nonacademic general students," these were seniors, anything but college-bound. I thought they'd enjoy true-life action, so I gave each student a copy of a book on men and war called *God Is My Co-Pilot*. It was 8:05 in the morning, and I was not quite twenty-two years old.

A minute later a huge black kid named Pete stood and ceremoniously ripped the paperback in half. "I ain't readin' this crap," he said, and let the pages flutter to the floor. The rest of the students, every one of them, immediately followed suit.

Now what? I wasn't going to be able to beat up thirty

kids, much as I would have liked to. And if I sent them to the principal's office I would expose myself as a wimpy disciplinarian. Talk about motivation! I had no clue, no training. The class looked at me with defiance, as if daring me to do anything.

In sheer desperation I pointed to Pete and called him Jack. "What's your thing, Jack?" I said.

He glared and narrowed his eyes. "Huh?"

"What do you do for a living that makes you good enough to rip up a man's book?"

"Mechanic," he said.

"Is that right?" I said. "An auto mechanic?"

He nodded. "Best in town."

"No kiddin'? What if I told you I don't believe a word you said?"

"'Bout what? I *am* a mechanic."

"About being the best in town."

"Ask anybody."

"How about you prove it?"

"Like how?"

"Well, I'll tell you what. Since you don't want to read any books, you're on tomorrow."

"On what?"

"You're the teacher," I said. "You bring a carburetor in here and teach this class. If you're the best, you ought to be able to teach us what you do."

"You kiddin' me?"

I stared him down, shaking my head.

"You got it," he said.

I should have been suspicious the next day when he showed up with a carburetor—still dripping gas—wrapped in a newspaper. It didn't hit me where he'd gotten it until I overheard another teacher later in the day complaining that something was missing from his engine.

Pete didn't wait for an introduction. He strode to the front, told me to sit down, and plopped the carburetor on the table. "Everybody shut up!" he said.

I never understood or cared much about auto mechanics

until Pete began. Suddenly, in his area of expertise, he was eloquent. He spoke with passion and knowledge. He not only knew his stuff, but he was also able to explain it.

Afterward I told him how well he had done and asked what he knew about race car carburetion. "I don't know, 'cept it's different."

"Find out and you'll be on again next month."

"I don't have no race cars to work on."

"I don't care where you find out. Try the library."

He swore. "I ain't been to no library and I ain't goin' to no library."

"I don't care where you get your information, but find out and teach us."

I asked another kid, who said he was a pool player, to demonstrate for us. I brought in a small pool table, and this guy, who was flunking his math classes, told us more about angles and drag and friction than I had ever known. I challenged him to study up on some of the great pool players for his second presentation. One of the girls talked about her work in a local bakery. One of the hill kids told about trapping.

On Fridays I talked about morality and ethics and demonstrated what I knew of the martial arts so the kids would know who was really in charge. For the first thirty class days, I didn't do much of anything but listen to the kids talk about what they enjoyed the most.

When it was Pete's turn again, he showed up with note cards. I had said nothing about note cards. "What are you doing with those?"

"That lady in the library said they would help my presentation," he said. "You know they got a whole section on automotive down there? Now you want me to teach or what?"

Eventually, each student taught twice. Meanwhile, I was ordering books on their areas of interest. Soon they were reading and writing, two things I had said little about. Pete began carrying around a pocket dictionary, badgering me about any word he didn't recognize. He wound up going to Central State in Ohio.

Too many people who teach have no idea of the principle of teaching. The goal of education is to expand the mind. A person's mind cannot be expanded unless he or she is motivated. There are many ways to motivate a person, but there is only one underlying principle: raise expectations.

Almost without knowing it, I raised the expectations of those students. They saw themselves as losers, unmotivated, uncaring. When they were challenged to do something, to show off their expertise, they gained confidence and were even motivated to expand, to learn something more. Their expectations of themselves had been raised.

Beside that, I was also learning things about teaching I had never been taught in the classroom. Admittedly, much of it was theoretical and perhaps even esoteric, but it was eye-opening for me. I was learning that while there may be hundreds of ways to get something done—for instance, motivating a student—there was but one underlying principle: raise his or her expectations. Later I would apply that "hundreds of ways but just one principle" to my chosen area of expertise: Verbal Judo. For instance, there are hundreds of ways to calm someone down, but if you know the one underlying principle, "the one hoping to do the calming must project empathy," you can decide, case by case, which method best fits the principle for the person in question.

I'll get into all those principles and how to best implement them, but my point here is to show how my teaching consciousness was born. Though I was barely aware of it at the time, my most difficult, most challenging classroom full of rebels taught me more about teaching and communicating than I would learn until I became a cop.

4

Taking Crap with Dignity...and Style

THE KIDS IN that remedial reading class were part of what I call the Great Why Way. If you have children, you will go or have gone through this stage. It begins as early as age eleven and sometimes never ends. That kid you used to be able to advise and coach and direct suddenly becomes a Why Guy. He or she has become just like the street lizards the beat cops encounter every day. They question every statement, every command, even every suggestion. "May I see your license, please?" may sound like a perfectly legitimate request to you or me, but there's always someone who reacts not with "Sure, here it is," but with "Why? What'd I do?"

Society is full of these people, from your teenager to your spouse, your client, your subordinate, your neighbor. (There is more on these types of people, and others, in the next chapter.) We are forced to become persuaders, and no one is trained in persuasion. Until now. That's my goal. I want to expand your mind, and so I need you motivated. The fact that you're still reading is an indication that you have a desire and a certain expectation. I'm telling you, if I can do this, you can do it. If I can become a practitioner of

Verbal Judo, anyone can. If that raises your expectation, makes you believe you can learn and improve your skills and thus succeed, you're a motivated student.

THE GENTLE WAY

Verbal Judo begins with a habit of mind. In Japanese, *ju* means "gentle" and *do* means "way," thus *judo* means "the gentle way." That definition is a surprise to many who assume that the meaning of words like *judo* and *karate* must necessarily be warlike and aggressive. Even *karate*, which is widely associated with B movies full of violence and mayhem and all manner of death blows, literally means "open hand" or "empty hand." The martial arts are self-defense techniques, not kill mechanisms.

As you learn Verbal Judo (the gentle way of persuasion) through a series of absolute principles, you'll form new habits of mind that will guide you to becoming a consciously competent speaker. You'll discover that it's possible to have a good communication day every day.

Though I have carefully studied this for years and will present to you everything I know about it with all my educational principles in mind, it probably won't seem natural to you at first. That's because truly enlightened communication does not come naturally to anyone, at least not to anyone I've ever met. (Of course, I never met Gandhi.) Thus, I always warn people in my classes, "Never use words that rise readily to your lips, or you'll make the greatest speech you'll ever live to regret."

Remember that glib phrase George Bush was so fond of during his 1988 campaign? "Read my lips: no new taxes" seemed to just roll off his lips. It may be the greatest speech he lived to regret.

Because I teach you to be careful of the words that rise automatically to your lips, the Verbal Judo that you substitute will initially feel foreign to you. But as you gradually learn new thinking habits and corresponding language, they will eventually feel comfortable and become automatic. As you learn to choose and deliver your words for maximum effectiveness, you'll enjoy benefits beyond merely improved communication.

You'll find that you can remain calm, which is a particularly valuable art. If your antagonist can upset you, he owns you at some level. Even if you score an immediate "victory" by telling him off, he may own you later when the encounter is evaluated by your boss, in court, by your family, or wherever.

Cops often learn this the hard way. What they thought was a good arrest Friday night might be worthless in court Monday morning because of something they did or said. You'll get plenty of good and bad examples as we go on.

As a student of Verbal Judo, you'll also learn how to talk with people in such a way that neither of you loses face. This is crucial because personal face is always a fighting issue, whether the conflict occurs on the street or in the boardroom, in court or in the bedroom.

You'll also discover surprisingly simple phrases that establish immediate empathy. And you'll recognize conflict as a gift, a communication game that helps you learn to master yourself.

You'll soon be able to use words that immediately establish your credibility with strangers. With friends, family, and associates, you'll know what to say to strengthen relationships—especially when those bonds are under pressure. You'll even learn to talk smoothly to people with whom you totally disagree.

With Verbal Judo you will learn to get what you want by using the dual powers of mind-set and words. In essence, you can become a master of communication, both internal and external. This is no small accomplishment. Verbal Judo will allow you to fulfill your dreams and wishes without creating stress, frustration, or conflict.

In the meantime, you'll never again mentally beat up on yourself by moaning, "Why didn't I keep my big mouth shut?"

THE SUCKER PUNCHES OF LIFE

The secretary habitually lies and says the boss is in a meeting and can't take your call. The youthful put-down artist advises you to "chill out and get a life." The alleged friend suggests, "We've got to get together for lunch," but is always booked when you try.

Welcome to some of the standard sucker punches of life. And this is the little stuff! As with cops, the most dangerous weapon you carry is a cocked tongue. It can fire off a sentence that will stall or even ruin your career. It can start a fight in the street (and I have the scars to prove it). It can send you to divorce court (and I have those scars too).

While your body can usually recover from physical blows, the bad news is that emotional wounds inflicted by words are likely to remain in your memory forever.

The good news is that with training, you can learn to take crap with dignity and style. Few of us can claim that there isn't any such garbage coming our way. The question is not whether such attacks will come, but how you will deal with them. Are you going to handle them with grace and ease, feeling in the end that everyone benefited? Or will you come away feeling like a wimp, a bully, a loser, an idiot—or all of the above?

If you learn to take taunts or criticism effectively, you won't even have to worry about other Verbal Judo techniques, such as deflecting. While such skills are important and good, they aren't always necessary. With practice you can learn to take insults with so much finesse and panache that they either disappear or never touch you.

As the Confucian philosopher Sun-tzu put it, "To win one hundred victories in one hundred battles is not the highest skill. To subdue the enemy without fighting is the highest skill."

A modern example of this surfaced in the 1990 Texas gubernatorial campaign of Clayton W. Williams, Jr. In Texas the word *bubba* is a generic term used to describe redneck good ol' boys, and Williams was accused of pandering to the bubba vote. Rather than argue the point, he gleefully responded, "I *am* bubba!" That approach turned the tide and almost won him the election.

The first step in learning to deal with verbal attacks is to acknowledge that crap is being flung. The second step is to admit it is being flung at you. Then congratulate yourself. It's okay to be questioned, heckled, or even attacked. If you are willing to take it, you should be commended. The only way to avoid criticism is either to live in a capsule or spend your whole life trying to please everyone. That means playing it safe, surrounding yourself with sycophants, taking few responsibilities, and doing what other people tell you to do.

The moment you have an idea and try to persuade others to move in concert with you, you have invited disagreement. The more intensely you live, the more you choose to make a difference in the world, the more you create vital, as opposed to insipid, relationships, then the more open you are to whacks and bumps and bruises. That's the only path to honest, bottom-line communication.

Who wins the highest office in a democratic society? It's the one who has made a career of attracting verbal abuse, deflecting it, and surviving in the biggest crap-taking business of all: politics.

Want a taste of that? Get yourself appointed to any committee whose job it is to improve the status quo. Eventually you'll meet dissension and resistance because most people oppose change. They will fight to keep things the way they are.

It isn't just politicians and do-gooders who need advanced communication skills. Professionals such as law enforcement officers, teachers, health care providers, salespeople, service personnel—typical groups I am invited to train—are learning how to use words to get what they need from others.

People in these groups take verbal abuse for a living, and all of us do at one time or another. Parents certainly do.

And so do students, homemakers, everybody. The key then is to learn how to avoid tumbling, or how to fall with grace without getting hurt. You will be attacked; there's little question of that. The real question is whether you'll become a stronger, more flexible person or become more of a wimp.

Even as an expert in this area, I face the temptation to fall into the traps all the time. Recently I was driving to my office in Albuquerque when a kid who looked to be about seventeen drove past me as I entered the parking lot and just missed sideswiping my new pickup. I was furious. When he got out of his car, I growled, "Where'd you learn to drive?"

He looked at me calmly and announced, "Texas!" Then he disappeared.

By the time I got into my office I realized I had met an unconscious competent. He was a master of Verbal Judo and didn't even know it. He had stopped me with one word. Had he turned on me and matched my tone with a "What's it to you, you SOB?" we'd have soon been in a shouting match and who knows what else? Three times his age, twice his size, and trained in martial arts and police tactics, I could have seriously injured him and ruined my life.

But he hadn't even appeared upset when I yelled at him. Not only did he not seem to mind the attack, but he also appeared to enjoy it.

That's how ancient samurai warriors viewed their battles. They lived for them. They were trained to see warfare as a joy and conflict, as a sign that they were drawing more energy. The issue for them was not winning or losing—or even living or dying. The issue was bravely engaging, fighting with great style, learning from the encounter. And because the warriors welcomed warfare, they were less likely to be tense while engaged in it, less likely to shut down and forget their training.

Clayton "I *am* bubba" Williams and the reckless teenage driver shared an ease about confrontation. They were loose enough to respond with a simple, truthful answer that stopped their detractors cold. Williams did it with three words. The teen flattened me with one.

The secret is simple: It's okay if someone insults, resists, or attacks you. Laugh it off. Show that it has no meaning, no sting. If you fight back and resist the affront, you give it life and credibility. If you defend yourself, you invite counterattack.

Look what happened when Richard Nixon declared, "I am not a crook." If, instead of lying or defending himself, he had early on merrily told the truth, without anger or defensiveness or sarcasm, he might actually have survived politically. Imagine if he had said, "We got caught in a stupid move and we're going to make it right."

When I train cops around the country I find that black officers are usually more adept at letting insults roll off them. Why? Probably because they have had to survive in a world that constantly attacks them. Many of them grew up playing a game called Dozens.

Dozens teaches kids to handle verbal abuse. They learn looseness and agility in conversational play. The worst taunts imaginable, usually insults of each other's mothers, are hurled back and forth. "Yo' mama so stupid, she heard it was chilly outside, so she brought out a bowl!" "Oh yeah? Well, *yo'* mama so old she was born before slavery!" Sometimes a shorthand version of Dozens is the simple insulting phrase, "Yo' mama!"

What happens is that one player finally takes it personally and reacts in anger. He loses face and loses credibility. He also loses the game and is laughed at. By playing Dozens again and again, a black kid eventually catches on that an attack carries only the weight he allows it to. He learns that if he makes no big deal of even an insult to his mother there's no incentive for anyone to keep insulting him. He has learned to effortlessly, eloquently, and effectively disarm the cocked tongue.

5

The Nice, the Difficult, and the Wimp

SOME NATIVE AMERICANS, primarily the Sioux and the Navaho, will look you in the eye under only two conditions: Either they happen to be your blood brother or sister (highly unlikely) or they're measuring you for the kill. Other Native Americans see a handshake as a sign of deference, and thus will offer a weak open hand and close it gently, considering the vigorous gripping of a hand as a sign of aggression and superiority. Many Hispanics are taught not to even glance directly into people's eyes, an act considered by several cultures as snooping on the soul. Many Asians still observe the gesture of looking at one's shoes as a sign of respect.

As our society becomes more culturally diverse, whites are quickly being displaced as a majority. There is a rising chorus of minority voices and an incalculable number of intercultural do's and don't's to be learned.

To calm someone brought up in the Western world, most people know to get outta his face and outta his space. Back off, give him some room. Yet when dealing with someone from the Middle East, say, an Egyptian or a Iranian, backing away from him would be the equivalent of telling Jewish

American Princess jokes at the local synagogue. Moving away from a Middle Easterner tells him he is unworthy of your respect. Better to move closer, to speak reassuringly, to tell him, "It's going to be all right." Even a slight touch on the shoulder will do wonders.

How do we keep track of all this? Move in? Step back? Look a person in the eye? Look at his feet? It could make you crazy.

In Southern California they've got a real challenge. In Garden Grove, a medium-sized city about fifty miles south of Los Angeles, at least thirty-three different languages represent more than one hundred distinct cultures. Shopkeepers, gas station attendants, anybody who deals with the public, has to routinely deal with all these groups.

I've warned cops that if they serve even a minor felony warrant in a Thai or Laotian home they've got to be extremely careful not to step or stand on the threshold. In those homes the spirits of departed ancestors are believed to reside in the cracks of the threshold, and someone stepping or standing on that crack gives the resident the right to slap the offender upside the head. If you don't know the local customs and superstitions somewhere, it's better to politely ask, "May I come in? May I stand here? Do you mind if I . . . ?"

I don't even attempt to train people in the subtleties of handling all the different peoples in the world. That would be virtually impossible. You'll be happy to know that there is a far simpler method for effectively dealing with people. All you need know is that there are three basic types of people in the world, and each should be handled differently. These types cut across all cultures, races, nationalities, ages, and sexes.

There are Nice People, Difficult People, and Wimps.

If you're in a position of authority, Nice People will do what you ask them to do the first time you ask them. They like to cooperate. Tell a Nice Child to pick up his belongings, and he'll do it, probably right away. Tell a Nice Person to send in a payment, and the money arrives on time.

Nice People don't shake their fingers in the boss's face.

They don't complain to hotel managers that their room is too close to the elevator or not close enough. They don't send food back to the kitchen if it arrives slightly over or undercooked.

My grandfather was a Nice Person. If he was stopped by a cop, he'd do exactly what he was told, automatically, even if the cop was nasty about it. As an attorney, he believed in the law more than he cared about a particular officer's execution of it. My grandfather would never give a cop any trouble, let alone anyone else. He considered it more egregious to make a scene than to make a point.

Nice People often have such a hard time saying no or sticking up for their rights that entire books have been written about them, such as *Co-Dependent No More, The Doormat Syndrome,* and *Women Who Love Too Much.*

Nice People are not your problem, but it's still wise to treat them as if they're important. If you don't treat them well, they may do what you want but will feel rotten about it. You'll lose credibility with them and gradually they'll stop supporting you. Besides, just because they are cooperative is no reason to take advantage of them or take them for granted. Treating them with respect is right because it's right. So few people are cooperative that you have to cultivate and cherish the ones who are.

I don't fit in the Nice People category. Maybe you don't either. I happen to be one of the Difficult People. By definition Difficult People will not do what you tell them the first time you ask. It doesn't matter how diplomatic you are. It's simply not in their nature to say, "Oh yes." Their nature makes them say, "Why? What for?" Difficult People are as eager to argue a point as Nice People are to cooperate.

Difficult People are also often persnickety. They would have no hesitation about interviewing a teacher before they decided whether to enroll in a class. They think nothing of insisting that a merchant pay shipping on an item that was out of stock when they visited the store.

Remember Meg Ryan's Sally to Billy Crystal's Harry in the movie *When Harry Met Sally?* When Harry orders his meal, he says, "I'll have the number three." Sally says, "I'd like the chef's salad, please, with oil and vinegar on the side and apple pie à la mode. But I'd like the pie heated and I don't want the ice cream on top. If not, then no ice cream, just whipped cream, but only if it's real. If it's out of a can, then nothing."

"Not even the pie?" asks the waitress.

"No," says Sally, "just the pie but then not heated."

You can be sure that if the waitress had told Sally it was impossible to substitute strawberry for vanilla, Sally would have wanted to know why.

The word *why* throws people off, especially those not accustomed to having their orders challenged. When I first went on the streets as a cop, the word really irritated me. It seemed it was all I heard.

"Step over here a minute please, sir."

"Why? What'd I do?"

"May I see your driver's license?"

"Why?"

In those days I barked, "Because I asked for it," acting pompous and inviting a tough time.

Gradually I learned that *why* is the bottom line in America. That little word can be one of the most powerfully destructive or constructive words in any language. It is the Horatio Alger question that built this country and tore down the Berlin Wall. Thirty years of the cold war didn't do that. It was the word *why*. The Soviet Union disintegrated when the Russian republics began asking, "Why should we take our orders from Moscow?"

Why is the word that created everything from lunar landings to drive-through hamburger joints. It is the word that irritates parents more than any other, but it also is a sign that children are growing up and maturing.

"Why?" is the most American question there is. The second and third most American questions—and sure to infuriate—are "Who do you think you are to tell me what to do?" and "Where do you get your authority?"

The fourth all-American inquiry, which, if you can answer it, will help you deal with the first three, is "What's in it for me?"

When Difficult People challenge your authority, it is usually pointless to explain why you've asked them to do something. They may not even care that you are authorized to make your request. They may not even care about the consequences of failing to obey. But they are always interested in how the deal might benefit them. When I want voluntary compliance from a Difficult Person, I explain early on what's in it for him. As clearly and specifically as I can, I show him what he has to gain. Only when that doesn't work will I tell him what he stands to lose.

With kids it may be useful to inform them that if they keep their room clean every day they will be entitled to a long session of unsupervised Nintendo madness. If that's not enough incentive, remind them they will forfeit the same privilege if they insist on living in a pigsty.

The first principle of physical judo is to not resist your opponent. Instead, move with him and redirect his energy. Ignoring or dismissing a question is the same as resisting it. In Verbal Judo you do not try to shut out pesky questioning of your authority, reasons, or methods. It's important to always answer, rather than dismiss the question when someone asks *why*.

Instead, leap into those questions, turn them into outrageous opportunities. See questions as invitations to explain yourself, to tell what you do, to fill someone in on your views. Here's the chance to educate a person, to win his respect, and provide him with deeper understanding so he won't go away angry.

Say a library patron demands to know why citizens have to pay late-return penalties on materials that are public property. The librarian could snap that such penalties are meant to discourage tardiness and discourtesy and thus keep the materials available to a wider range of people. But that tone would insult the patron. How much better to calmly explain with a smile that the fines pay for videotapes, lecture programs, books, periodicals, and many other wonderful things the patrons enjoy without charge.

I stopped being irritated at Difficult People asking "Why?" all the time when I realized that I am one of them. They're my kind of people! When someone says, "No, that's wrong. You can't do that to me. What gives you the right to tell me what to do?" I get interested. That's a challenge. I actually enjoy it now when Difficult People look me in the eye and say, "Why do I have to do that?" It gives me the opportunity to explain why it's in their best interest to comply.

Difficult People built this country. We need to allow room in our system for them and their questions. If you can carry this mind-set with you, one that appreciates other people's sense of dignity and self-worth, curiosity and healthy suspicion, you'll never be upset by people who initially challenge your authority. You'll never back away from fussbudgets who nag you to do something especially for them when it's not in your repertoire of services. You'll never go home with a knot in your stomach because you were asked to explain the reasons for what you did or didn't do.

There's a big payoff in all this: When you shift from resisting to appreciating and even welcoming Difficult People, things become interesting and less tense.

The toughest bird of all is the Wimp. Wimps are the ones who sound like Nice People but are closet Difficult People. To your face they say, "Oh yes," "I agree," "You're right." They may even compliment you on your words, ideas, or even clothes. They've got the courtesy rap down cold. But later they get you back, in the back, baby.

These backstabbers are customers or colleagues who act friendly and pretend all is well with your relationship. Then they bitch about you to your boss, to their friends, and to anyone else who'll listen (and who doesn't love to listen to bad mouthing?). These are the people who will file lawsuits and hire a lawyer to do their fighting for them. If you've ever had a complaint that took you by surprise, you can bet it came from a Wimp, someone who didn't have the guts to tell you to your face that he had a problem. Generally you can assume that you didn't handle the Wimp properly when you first encountered him or you didn't recognize him as a Wimp and see the grievance coming. Admittedly, most Wimps are good at Wimpdom, making them hard to detect.

Wimps do not like authority. They hate being told what to do. On the other hand, they don't have the guts to challenge you. Wimps want revenge. They feel the need to even the score. These are the ones who snipe from the corner, sitting in meetings and making disparaging remarks just loud enough to be heard by a few and generate laughs of derision.

I frequently face Wimps in my classes, yes even among cops. I have found the best way to deal with them is to strip them of their camouflage. Not honest enough to be straightforward Difficult People—who are much easier to deal with—Wimps usually want to hide behind other people. Often they sit in the back of a room or against the wall or near a pillar or post.

When I'm teaching Verbal Judo and I hear people mutter, "That's a bunch of garbage," I don't let it pass.

I say, "Excuse me, what was that you said? I'd like to know." When they try to wave me off or laugh it away, I persist. "No, tell me so I can speak to it."

The Wimp has been stripped of his cover and now he has to put up or shut up. Now he can either make a legitimate point, ask a question, or shut up. And if he shuts up he has lost credibility with his peers. If nothing else, that eliminates the sniping.

Many think it's best to ignore Wimps, but that's just another form of resisting them. Ignored or resisted, they grow stronger. The basic principle here is to confront them honestly. They immediately weaken.

Resist the urge to gossip about these people or snipe back at them. Those are Wimp techniques, and they are often better at them than you are, unless you too are a Wimp.

Outside of my training sessions, in private, I'm even more direct with Wimps. Notice that when I'm flushing them out of their cover in the class setting I'm not embarrassing them. I'm letting them embarrass themselves. If they have a good point or something constructive to say or ask, they can. I haven't put them down or challenged them. I've merely courteously asked them to repeat their comment or question because I missed it. Privately, however, I might be more straightforward. "I understand what you're doing," I'll say. "If you continue, we're going to have a problem. I won't put up with this."

The pure Wimp, true to form, will immediately back down and even apologize. I still watch them like hawks, however.

Exposure is totally unsettling to Wimps. Once you've blown their chicken-hearted covers, by and large they will leave you alone. They'll either realize that their tactics don't work with you and give up, or they'll find someone else to bother.

Learning to identify and distinguish the Nice, the Difficult, and the Wimp is a basic first step in your journey of mastering Verbal Judo.

6

Eleven Things Never to Say to Anyone (And How to Respond If Some Idiot Says Them to You)

1. "COME HERE!"

Ironically, this command actually means "Go away," especially when said by an intimidating authority figure. Many street people automatically translate the phrase as "Run like the devil!"

To you and me, "Come here!" is vaguely threatening. It says, "You haven't obeyed me, so now I'm ordering you to move when I want you to move."

I learned in police work that it's much more effective to casually approach a person and say, "Excuse me, but I need to chat with you a second," or even "Could I chat with you a second?" I gave the other party the feeling that he had some choice, but my implication was clear.

It's best to control the location for such encounters. Samurai warriors cautioned their students to never let an op-

47

ponent pick the fighting terrain. The reason was simple: Those who didn't choose found themselves with the sun in their eyes and/or on loose ground.

If someone with no authority orders *you* to "Come here!" and doesn't seem to have legitimate reasons, ask, "Why? If you don't get a satisfactory answer, become a street person and run like the devil.

2. "YOU WOULDN'T UNDERSTAND."

I don't know about you, but I find this phrase so insulting that I can almost hear the comma and then "stupid" implied at the end. No matter who this is said to, it puts the listener off. Better to say, "This might be difficult to understand, but . . ." or "Let me try to explain this . . ."

There's no harm in warning people that what you're about to say is complicated and that it's okay if they don't get it at first. You can even put the onus on yourself: "I hope I can explain this . . ." Just don't prejudge their ability to comprehend. And certainly don't whip them in advance for what may be your failure to communicate.

If you're being pressed to reveal something you don't want to reveal, avoid the convenient lie that the person wouldn't understand. Just say, "I'd rather not answer that," or the more emphatic, "I'm not willing to answer that."

If someone brushes *you* off with "You wouldn't understand," insist, "Yes I would. Try me. I want to help."

3. "BECAUSE THOSE ARE THE RULES."

That phrase would make just about anybody want to throw up. But if you're enforcing rules that exist for good reasons, don't hesitate to explain them. Your audience might not agree, but at least they will have been honored with an answer. For instance, if you tell children they have to go to bed at a certain time and they demand to know why, explain that

they will be less cranky and able to have more fun the next day
if they get adequate sleep. Tell them that you need their help
in doing your job as a parent. "It's my responsibility to bring
up healthy, happy kids. You do your part, and I'll do mine."

If you fall back on "Because those are the rules," you'll
be judged an insensitive, uncaring oaf. It will appear you are
more concerned with your own authority than with the other
person's welfare. You may be told, "So what? The rules are
wrong."

If all you can do is to repeat that "rules are rules and
those are the rules," your listener knows you're weak and
can't support your order with logic. When you're desperate
you'll find yourself saying, "I don't have to explain; I'm the
boss [mother, father, authority, one giving the orders]." But
if you can put the rules or policies in context and explain
how they contribute to everyone's well-being, you not only
help people understand, you help them save face. And you're
also much more likely to gain voluntary compliance.

Should someone—who hasn't had the good fortune to
read this book—tell *you* "Because those are the rules," say,
"Could you please tell me why this rule was created? It doesn't
make sense to me, and if you could help me understand why
it was made, it would be much easier for me to follow."

4. "IT'S NONE OF YOUR BUSINESS."

Here is the slam-dunk of verbal abuse. It's usually said by a
frustrated parent, but it's occasionally heard among friends
too. The phrase angers people because it brands them as
outsiders and brusquely cuts them off. It also exposes you as
someone who doesn't have a good reason for answering the
question. It makes it seem that you have no power behind
your position.

Rather than saying, "It's none of your business," explain
why the information cannot be revealed. You can usually do
this without revealing more than you want to. If it's a con-
fidential matter, say why. For instance, "The parties involved

would not want me to say anything without their knowledge or permission, and I want to honor that—you understand."

If you're simply uncomfortable revealing something, just admit that, rather than making the other person feel like a jerk. Telling him it's none of his business leads only to conflict. Have you ever heard someone reply, "You're right. It's none of my business and I shouldn't have asked"? No, he usually reacts angrily and keeps badgering until you blurt out something you shouldn't have.

If someone barks at *you* that something is none of your business, and you disagree, gently but firmly point out, "It *is* my business, and here's why."

5. "WHAT DO YOU WANT *ME* TO DO ABOUT IT?"

What a cop-out! The pseudo question, almost always accompanied by sarcasm, is seen as an evasion of responsibility. It's also a sign that you're exasperated. It's often said by untrained sales clerks in response to complaints, but it's also heard among friends, spouses, and co-workers at the ends of their ropes.

When you say "What do you want *me* to do about it?" you can count on two problems: the one you started with and the one you just created by appearing to duck responsibility.

Rather, offer to help sort out the problem and work toward a solution. If it truly is not in your area of responsibility, point the complainer to the right department or person. If you're unable or unqualified to assist and you haven't a clue how to help the person, nicely say so and apologize. You didn't do anything wrong, but an apology almost always gains you an instant ally. No one wants you to feel bad for something that's not your fault.

Say, "I'm sorry. I really don't know what to tell you or what else to recommend, and I wish I did. I'd like to help, but I can't." A concerned tone will enhance your credibility and convey that you're not secretly just trying to pass the buck.

If someone asks *you* "What do you want *me* to do about

it?" start by explaining, "I want you to listen to me and help me." Then politely explain exactly how the person can help.

6. "CALM DOWN!"

I have a lot of fun with this intrinsically contradictory command, in my seminars, especially with police officers but also with service personnel. I scrunch up my face into a mean grimace and ask them how calming it is when I say (shouting now), "Calm down!"

The command flat out doesn't work. In fact, it almost always makes people more upset. If you've ever tried this on your friends or family, you know. "Calm down!" is criticism of people's behavior and implies that they have no right to be upset. Rather than reassuring them that things will improve—which should be your goal—you have created a new problem. Not only is there the matter they were upset about to begin with, but now they need to defend their reaction to you.

Rather, put on a calm face and demeanor, look the person in the eye, touch him gently if appropriate, and say, "It's going to be all right. Talk to me. What's the trouble?"

If someone says "Calm down!" to *you*, say, "Look, I'm obviously not calm and there are reasons for it. Let's talk about them." That should open the door for that person to help, but if he doesn't respond in a more meaningful way, further discussion is probably unwise. And if you're not calm, it's probably better to leave.

7. "WHAT'S YOUR PROBLEM?"

This snotty, useless phrase turns the problem back on the person needing assistance. It signals that this is a "you versus me" battle rather than an "us" discussion. The typical reaction is defensive. "It's not *my* problem; *you're* the problem!"

The problem with the word *problem* is that it makes people feel deficient or even helpless. The word can transport them back to grade school when they felt misunderstood and underrated. Nobody likes to admit he has a problem. People prefer to think of solutions. "What's your problem?" makes them feel as if they've already failed.

Rather, say, "What's the matter? How can I help?" Then you can start a real discussion of the issue.

If someone is unenlightened enough to ask *you* "What's your problem?" say, "It's not a problem, it's just something I need to discuss. Can we talk?"

8. "YOU NEVER..." OR "YOU ALWAYS..."

These absolute generalizations are lies. Is it true that a child *never* cleans up his room? (Okay, bad example. That may be true!) Is it true that your spouse is "*always* late"? Accusatory generalizations are rarely true and indicate that you have both lost perspective *and* will soon lose the attention of your listener.

Tell someone he never listens to you and he will either remind you of several times when he has or he will be tempted to spitefully prove you right and ignore you. You also make him angry and leave him feeling there is no way he can ever please you.

Better to turn the burden upon yourself and seek his help. "When you are late without calling, it makes me feel as if you don't care about me or my schedule." That should elicit an apology or at least an explanation. But if you jumped in with "You never call..." you're more likely to be reminded of the three times in the last month when he *did* call.

If someone uses such absolute phrasing to you, see if you can see his point. Say, "I know it seems I never help out, because often I don't. But let's talk about it. Is that the real issue or are you upset about something else?"

9. "I'M NOT GOING TO SAY THIS AGAIN."

That is almost always a lie on the face of it, because what usually follows the above phrase? The thing you just said you weren't going to say again! And you will probably say it again and again. This threat traps you, because if you're really not going to repeat yourself, you're left with one option: action. If you're not prepared to act, you lose credibility.

If you *are* prepared to act, you have tipped off your adversary and he can plan to react to or subvert you. Better to not reveal all your options at once.

If you need to emphasize the seriousness of your words, say, "It's important that you understand this, so let me say it again. And please listen carefully."

If someone tells *you* "I'm not going to say it again," just answer with sincerity, "Okay, I got it."

10. "I'M DOING THIS FOR YOUR OWN GOOD."

That is guaranteed to turn any listener into an instant cynic. No one believes it. It begs the sarcastic comeback, "Oh yessssss. Sure, I bet."

If what you are doing really *is* for the other person's benefit, show him that. Offer reasons. Give concrete examples of how his life will improve because of what you're doing. Just as I encourage cops to tell perpetrators to surrender early so they don't have to spend the night in jail, away from their own table and hot food and loved ones, there is a benefit that can be pointed to for anyone you're trying to encourage to do something—for his own good.

If someone tells *you* "I'm doing this for your own good," ask for specifics. If what he says doesn't match your notion of what constitutes your own good, say so. Remind the person, "No one knows me better than I do. I'm the best judge of what is for my own good, just as you're the best judge of what is for your own good."

11. "WHY DON'T YOU BE REASONABLE?"

Not once in my life has anyone come up to me and said, "You know what? I'm in left field today, totally irrational." People may know they're a little forgetful or flaky or out of it, but they're not going to admit to being unreasonable. So you're only inviting conflict with a question like this.

Instead, allow people to become more reasonable by being reasonable with them. Use the language of reassurance, saying things like "Let me see if I understand your position," and then paraphrasing their own words. That not only assures you that you're hearing them correctly, but it also enables them to see their own view as you see it. That approach starts to absorb people's tension and makes them feel your support. Then you can help them think more logically and less destructively, without making the insulting charge implied in the question.

If someone asks *you* "Why don't you be more reasonable?" force yourself to slow down. Take a deep breath and in a slow, thoughtful, nonthreatening voice, say, "I'm being as reasonable as I know how, and with any luck, I'll get better. But apparently I see the issue differently than you do."

You will have deflected the attempt to put you down without further antagonizing the person.

If you can begin cutting these eleven examples of fightin' words from your vocabulary, you will take giant strides in your mastery of Verbal Judo, the gentle art of gaining voluntary compliance through empathic persuasion.

7

The Crucible of the Street

WHEN I LANDED a teaching job at Emporia State University in Kansas, I tried to keep a hand in both the physical and the academic worlds, which made me a strange bird. I wasn't your typical professor who practiced judo and tae kwon do karate on the side and rode with the local cops as a reserve in his spare time. My colleagues thought I was nuts.

After ten years I had just about had it with the urbane atmosphere of the campus. I was on so many committees I was meeting-ed to death. When I was finally assigned to a committee whose sole purpose was to oversee the work of the other committees, I was near the end of my rope. That's when I got serious about the reserve program at the local police department.

As soon as I started doing "ride-alongs" and training on the job, I fell in love with police work and knew I needed to get away from college teaching. I was becoming obnoxious at the university, trying to tell my colleagues how they didn't really know anything about communication skills, and that the cops were the real experts. When I finally made the break, they were probably relieved to see me go.

The very first night I was out by myself, I found I did not know how to communicate. I stopped a car after midnight for going through several stop signs at high speed. As I shone my flashlight inside the car, I noticed marijuana all over the floor. "You, sir," I snapped, "step out!"

The man grabbed the steering wheel with arms as big as my legs and snarled, "I ain't gettin' out!" He added a few choice profanities, and I was stunned. My students sure never talked to me that way! My children didn't talk to me that way. I couldn't remember a sentence put that forcefully to my face.

I didn't know what to say, so I just repeated my command. And he said, "I ain't gonna do it!"

Now what? I stood there in my brand-new police boots, looking good. My uniform was clean and crisply pressed. I had a snazzy, all-weather grip on my stainless steel .357 magnum. I was rocking back and forth on 210 pounds stretched fairly taut over six feet two inches, and I was feeling in shape. Even my patrol car was looking good. Everything was looking good, but I was just standing there rocking back and forth, back and forth, and nothing was happening.

So I came up with the worst sentence you can come up with. It rose effortlessly to my lips. "I'm not going to tell you again, sir. Step out!"

The man just looked at me and said, "Why don't you stop talking about it and do something about it?"

I figured his advice was probably better than mine, so with him calling the shots, I acted. With my black belts in tae kwon do and combat judo, I know how to lay hands on people, so if that's what he was begging for, I was ready and willing to comply. I'd been doing that all my life. I ripped the car door open, pulled him out, and threw him to the ground. I cuffed him up and dragged him to jail. You can bet I felt pretty good about it too.

About an hour later I ran into somebody who gave me more verbal hassle, and I only asked him twice. See, I was learning. He resisted so I threw him down, cuffed him up, and took him to jail. I was made for this job. Things were working my way.

About quarter of seven in the morning, I was putting the patrol car away beneath the police department when the dispatcher radioed me that there was a drunk banging on the windows. "Could you move him on down the street?"

Could I move him down the street? Man, you're talkin' to John Wayne here. I went up and asked the drunk only once. I said, "Sir, would you cooperate with me and move on down the street?" When he snarled unintelligibly at me, I threw him down, cuffed him up, and took him to jail. It was the wrong night to be fooling with the toughest new cop on the beat. I went home feeling good.

At about 11:00 A.M. I was awakened by a call from the chief of police, who asked if I would come to his office. "I want to chat with you." I dressed quickly. Though I was thirty-five, not twenty-one, I was still so brain-damaged that I went down there thinking I was about to get a commend-ation because of my good night.

As soon as I walked in I noticed that the chief's voice had changed from the voice I had heard over the phone. "Take a look through the one-way glass into my waiting room and then sit yourself down!"

There were two couples, big as gorillas, sitting on hard chairs, clearly not pleased. "Who are they?" I said.

The chief said, "No, George, that's my question. Who are those parents and why are they here complaining about your behavior with their sons? What in the world happened out there last night?"

Suffice it to say my explanations weren't good enough. The chief impressed upon me that I had gone about my work all wrong, that there was a better, more conciliatory way to do things. "You've got to reason with people, George."

"Well, Chief, what should I have said? A man tells me, 'I ain't gonna do what you say,' what am I supposed to say? I want to be a good cop. Give me the words, and, by gosh, I'll use those phrases."

The sad fact was, he didn't have any phrases. He told me I should be more persuasive, more reasonable, and try other tactics, but I left with no concrete examples. All he said was, "Don't let it happen again." I went home, snapping like a Doberman. I'd come in for a letter of commendation and gone away with a condemnation, so I was not a happy camper.

The only thing I learned that night was that there was something I didn't know. I didn't have a clue to the goal of persuasion. That's why I teach it now. I don't teach reasoning, I don't teach argument, I don't teach debate. I don't even teach logic. I teach the lost art of persuasion, how to effect voluntary compliance.

Because of my frustration and the newspaper-and-phone approach used by Bruce Fair several days later, I soon began to learn more about communication on the streets than I ever had learned in a college classroom. It was clear that the vast majority of police work was verbal, not physical. Recent studies have shown that police work is 97 to 98 percent oral interaction. (It's even higher in most other professions.)

As I analyzed the verbal and nonverbal communication of the cops I worked with, patterns began to emerge. There were peacemakers and troublemakers, some officers who could end a brawl with a few choice words and others who virtually started fights by lumbering on to the scene as if ready to take on all comers.

Different cops used different styles, but the effective ones invariably employed the same profound and—I believed—definable principles I knew from the martial arts. I soon realized that these principles worked in all sorts of situations. They could help anybody get what he or she wanted—whether that meant arresting a thug without a fight or persuading a storekeeper to issue a refund. If I was right, the same principles would work on everything from soothing an angry boss to motivating an MTV addict to do her homework.

After five and a half years of police work, I went back to teach for a year at Emporia State. This time I stayed away from all the committees. I wanted books, students, a classroom, and to be left alone to teach. In my downtime, I began writing about the astounding communication tools used routinely by sharp street cops. An article I wrote in 1982 was published in *The FBI Bulletin*. To my amazement, more than six hundred letters poured in from all over the country, asking if I offered training in what I had begun to call Verbal Judo.

I was thunderstruck. I had published dozens of academic articles and had never heard from anyone. Now this little piece had generated response from law enforcement officials, educators, business executives, retailers, politicians, bureaucrats, even parents—all curious about how to apply the principles of Verbal Judo.

At the request of the police department in Abilene, Texas, I put together a Verbal Judo training course. If this stuff didn't work there, I knew they'd ride me out of town on a rail. I showed up ready to teach with a handful of rough notes and plenty of anxiety. Eight hours later I was still in town. No tar, no feathers, no fight, no rail. On the horizon, a whole new career.

THE UNCONSCIOUS COMPETENT

If you have had good days and bad days as a communicator, you are sometimes operating at the level of what I call unconscious competence. Without understanding why, you are sometimes effective.

Sgt. Bruce Fair, my Emporia, Kansas, partner and trainer, is the perfect example of an unconscious competent. He uses Verbal Judo without realizing it. Most of the time, he speaks brilliantly, but he has no idea why he's so effective. He's a gifted natural communicator.

The only problem with being an unconscious competent—especially if you're not as ingenious as Bruce—is that it can be dangerous. If you don't know why you're doing what you're doing, and you're depending on verbal instincts to get you through, you can make costly mistakes.

Verbal Judo teaches you to become consciously competent in both the use of words and in your nonverbal presence. If it's true that lack of communication is a major factor behind everything from ruined marriages to lost fortunes and world wars, verbal skills are crucial to the survival of society. If you've ever alienated anyone, burned any bridges (or even left them smoking), lost a promotion, or angered your mother-in-law, you have had communication problems.

I believe the greatest abuse today is verbal abuse, which is the basis for all child abuse, spouse abuse, drug abuse, and just about any other type of abuse you can think of. In fact I would argue that verbal abuse is far more prevalent than substance abuse in our country.

Tongue lashings are a major reason why people turn to drugs or alcohol. They don't feel worthy. Nowhere is this more evident than in our prisons. As part of my research when I was creating Verbal Judo, I interviewed more than two thousand prisoners in the Los Angeles area. I wanted to know what prisoners thought made a good cop, but I also talked to them about their lives in general. Let me tell you, our penal institutions are full of people who have been verbally, if not physically, abused all their lives. In their anger and rage, they set out to abuse others.

These prisoners—and sadly, millions of other people who are not criminals—have never heard words that would make them feel good about themselves. They've never heard gentle encouragement or praise. Their lives have been full of relentless taunts, criticisms, and put-downs.

That sort of verbal abuse lasts far longer than physical abuse. Ask yourself if you remember every spanking you received as a child. Now how about a specific, personal slam from someone you cared about? A wound inflicted by a hand or even a weapon will eventually heal and fade from memory. But old verbal wounds may never heal. Sticks and stones may break our bones, but words will break our hearts.

Words cut deeper and their wounds fester longer than traumas of the sword. That's why we need to be trained to speak effectively.

Parents and teachers taught us to read and write. But chances are they didn't train us to wisely communicate the spoken word. Our earliest verbal gaffes were countered with "Shut up and do as you're told."

Have you ever taken a class on how to speak with assurance and ease? Or one on presence under pressure? For most of us, it's a sad truth: No one has ever systematically trained us to speak effectively.

I earned a Ph.D. in English literature and never took one course in effective verbal communication. It wasn't part of my speech courses, which typically concentrated on how to present formal monologues or how to win debates. Let's face it: Those are highly artificial formats that bear no resemblance to real communication. In fact, one of the worst habits you can fall into when drawn into a verbal confrontation is to switch to a speech or debate mode.

Unless your parents were natural communicators, it's unlikely that you've learned to talk in a way that strengthens interpersonal relationships. That's the real goal of communication. Outside my own seminars in Verbal Judo and a few communication courses taught to valued employees in progressive corporation, I know of nowhere that communication to improve relationships is taught.

Similarly, there are few opportunities to learn how to receive and deflect insults, how to apologize, how to discipline, or how to praise. Yet it's in these critical communication areas that our power—and our weakness—lies. If we get any verbal instruction at all it's probably in assertiveness-training courses where we are taught to be confrontive and avoid being pushed around.

There may be value in that, but too many people come out of those courses more aggressive than assertive. They may get what they want, but they win few friends in the process. "A prospect sold against his will remains unsold still" goes the old sales adage.

Is it any wonder that some of our best-known and most respected communicators sometimes find themselves in big-league trouble because of how they choose their words? Even

as polished a communicator as daily talk show host Geraldo
Rivera found himself in a slugfest in August 1992 when a
verbal spat with an extremist escalated at a Ku Klux Klan
rally in Janesville, Wisconsin. Words failed the wordsmith,
he admitted later, " . . . and when he called me a spick and a
dirty Jew, threw something at me and kicked me, I punched
him in the mouth."

Look at our high-ranking politicians. On the floor of the
U.S. House of representatives, Robert Dornan and Thomas
Downey once got into a shoving match when Dornan
wouldn't apologize for calling Downey a "draft-dodging
wimp."

Even our alleged diplomats are notorious for speaking
without thinking. At a 1990 U.S.–China Trade Exposition in
Seattle, U.S. Ambassador to China James Lilley got suckered
into a yelling match with demonstrators and others who pro-
tested human rights abuses in China and Tibet.

Our diplomat was less than diplomatic when he shouted,
"Go back to China! You're a bunch of cowards!" Of course
the next day he had to eat crow and apologize. "It was a
mistake," he admitted. "I shouldn't have done it."

The talk show host, the congressmen, the ambassador,
and most of us are verbal disasters waiting to happen. No
one has taught us to communicate, particularly under pressure—when it's most important. You may have heard that
you shouldn't back someone into a corner, that you should
leave him a way out. But has anyone ever actually trained
you how to do that with what you say?

Verbal Judo is a series of simple, hard-nosed principles
and tactics that anybody can use, regardless of background.
You don't have to be a linguist to benefit from these martial
arts of the mind and mouth. Nor do you have to memorize
any complicated systems.

Frankly, I think you'll be thrilled with how simple, yet
thorough, my approach really is.

8

The Most Powerful Word in the English Language

ARE YOU LOOKING for an instant tension buster? A way to stop gossips and backstabbers dead in their slimy little tracks? Want to turn snarling antagonists into personalities as sweet and smooth as honey sliding from a jar?

The answer lies in one word, which represents the single most powerful concept in the English language: *empathy*.

To have empathy for someone does not mean to sympathize with him. It does not mean to love or even to like somebody. You don't have to approve of him. And you are certainly not required to agree with what he says or accept his invitation to Thanksgiving dinner.

Empathy has Latin and Greek roots. *Em,* from the Latin, means "to see through," and *pathy,* from the Greek, means "the eye of the other." So to empathize means to understand, to see through the eyes of another. It is the most crucial skill in both physical and Verbal Judo. That's because the moment you stop thinking like your spouse, you're headed for divorce court. The moment you stop thinking like your employer, you'd better start looking for another job. The moment you stop thinking like your friends, you'd better find yourself a new crowd to run with.

Empathy is the quality of standing in another's shoes and understanding where he's coming from.

Here is the bottom line of all communication: Empathy absorbs tension. It works every time. I have seen it even save a life.

The most dramatic example of this I have ever witnessed occurred one cold, windy night two years into my police career. I answered a call about a guy threatening to commit suicide. I had been on another call, and when I arrived I found a bunch of policemen standing around a man lying nude in a bathtub full of water. His toe was hooked to an electric heater, which he was threatening to jerk into the tub. It would, of course, have electrocuted him before our eyes.

"You pigs don't understand!" he screamed. "I want to kill myself!"

The officers pleaded with him, "C'mon, friend, you don't want to do that. You've got your whole life ahead of you. Things will look better tomorrow."

The only problem with that is that the guy knew better. He was the one with the problems: money, love, job, whatever. And Murphy's Law tells us things aren't going to be better tomorrow. A guy talking suicide thinks Murphy was an optimist anyway.

One of the officers turned to me and said, "This is your beat. You handle it."

I pulled another cop close and whispered, "Find the fuse box and cut off the power."

Meanwhile, I turned to the guy in the tub. Despite what he had said, I believed he was looking for a way out of his predicament. If he really wanted to die, he'd have killed himself. He wanted to be listened to, and now he needed to save face. Instead of trying to talk him out of frying himself in the tub, I decided to move *with* him. That meant I had to try to think like him. I quickly contemplated what it must be like to face imminent bathtub electrocution. It struck me as an especially horrible way to go.

I said, "You know, it's really too bad that of the hundred and five ways you can kill yourself, friend, you've picked the hundred and fifth most painful. You think it's going to be quick, right? You think all you have to do is pull the heater in the tub and you're gone. Let me tell you something. Research shows that death by electrocution in water can take anywhere from eight to twelve minutes—minutes of excruciating pain.

"You're going to smell your hair burning. You're going to see the water bubbling and boiling, your skin peeling back from your knuckles, your sternum split. If you think life's been tough up to now, friend, you've got eight to twelve minutes to consider real toughness. You have never felt such pain."

I paused as it became clear they were having trouble finding the fuse box or figuring how to cut the power. "It's a shame," I said. "There are a hundred and four easier and more efficient ways to do it. Why don't you step out of that tub and I'll tell you about them. Some are so quick you're gone before you know it."

It may seem that telling someone how to kill himself is anything but empathetic, but it was the only way I knew how to walk in the guy's shoes. And it worked. Just before they cut the electricity, he sprang out of that tub.

The truth is, I don't know how many ways there are to kill yourself. And I know very little about death by electrocution, except I understand it's pretty quick. I know I'm not right about the eight to twelve minutes, but squatting there in uniform next to a desperate man, I must have looked and sounded like the world's authority on the subject.

Okay, I was lying, but because I tried to empathize with the guy, I got in sync with him. He listened because I was working with him, trying to help him—if not to live then at least to die with less pain. He thought he wanted to kill himself; I promised I could help him get the job done better.

Admittedly, lying and trickery are not things that easily transfer into your everyday relationships. I don't recommend them. In this case, however, subterfuge was the only thing I could think of to empathize with the man. Though my story was fake, my concern was genuine, and he sensed it. My goal was to help him. Because I focused on him and his predicament, I was able to choose language that allowed him to see the situation as he hadn't seen it before.

He wanted to be understood.

I am not a social worker. I was never the best cop in the world. But I can try to understand. And then, by the way I use language and tone, I can buy someone another twenty-four to forty-eight hours. That's enough time for a man to have a cup of coffee and chat with a professional—somebody trained in helping him reconsider his life.

What I did for that guy is what police officers, teachers, parents, ministers, and others do all the time. We help people think as they would a day or two later, without the influence of fear or depression or temporary brain damage they bring to the situation.

A friend told me of a rash decision by his son that could have resulted in a regrettable act. In a typical circle of gossip, the boy's girlfriend heard some things he was supposed to have said about her. She called to break up with him. He was so hurt by being dumped that he fumed around the house, threatening to say about her the very things she had accused him of saying. "There are things I *could* tell about her," he wailed. "And since she already thinks that's what I've done, I might as well."

He went to the phone. "What are you doing?" his father asked.

"Evening the score," he said. "I'm going to tell a few of my friends things about her."

"Things said to you in confidence? Things between a boyfriend and girlfriend?"

"That's right." He was dialing.

"Could you give me just a minute?"

"Don't try to talk me out of this, Dad. She's already found me guilty, so I might as well do it."

"But you were innocent."

"That doesn't make any difference now."

"I can understand how hurt you are, being accused of something you didn't do by someone you care about. Do me a favor, will you? Give it twenty-four hours. If you still feel as strongly then, we'll talk again."

Notice the father didn't give him permission to spread gossip and break confidences if he still felt strongly the next day. He simply said they would talk again. He knew how quickly things change in kids' lives and that there were myriad reasons why his son might feel differently the next day.

The next morning, when he dropped his son off at school, the boy was still incensed. "Remember, you're giving me twenty-four hours and we'll talk again tonight." The boy nodded.

That evening the son was beaming. "She asked me to forgive her!" he announced. "She said she should have believed me, because when she called her friends they all said I had never broken my word or told stories behind her back."

The father resisted the temptation to take credit for keeping his son from having done just that. "So, you're back together?"

"Of course, Dad. Nothing can tear us apart."

This is the communication warrior's real service: staying calm in the midst of conflict, deflecting verbal abuse, and offering empathy in the face of antagonism. If you cannot empathize with people, you don't stand a chance of getting them to listen to you, much less accepting your attempts to help—sincere as you may be.

If you take a moment to think as another might be thinking, then speak with his perspective in mind, you can gain immediate rapport. Ill-fitting as his shoes may be, walk a few steps in them. Only then can you provide real understanding and reassurance. Only then can you help that person see the consequences of what he is doing or is about to do. Only then can you help him make enlightened decisions.

RODNEY KING

In the most famous police brutality case to date, Rodney King was kicked and clubbed at least fifty-six times on March 3, 1991, in Los Angeles. I wasn't there, but like just about every fully functioning citizen of North America, I've seen the video more times than I care to. I've heard the testimony that King was bludgeoned and kicked because he ignored verbal commands to get down and stay down, and apparently one jury was convinced the staggering, lumbering, dazed offender was a mortal threat to the officers.

I don't want to be naïve, and nothing I say here should be misconstrued as condoning the violence that broke out with the announcement of the first verdict, but I believe the police officers could have used words alone to take King in. I was training members of the LAPD at the time, and several of the officers on the scene that night were scheduled to be in my Verbal Judo class the week after the incident. When you've finished this book, ask yourself how you would have handled that dangerous, volatile situation, and see if you don't agree with me.

Fortunately, the vast majority of us will never find ourselves in such an explosive environment. Our verbal tussles are just as unsettling to us, however, so every tool we can employ, every skill we can master will only make our lives easier.

The highly trained adult professionals who resort to brute force no doubt consider themselves effective communicators, people who don't need to learn anything more about how to talk. That is the attitude of nearly every professional I teach, at least at the start. I find that it takes some in-your-face challenges to get them to sit up and listen. I need to earn the right to be heard, show that I've been where they are—in dangerous street situations—and convince them that there are indeed verbal skills that will make them better at their jobs.

Chances are that you, too, consider yourself a successful communicator. You have no doubt occasionally demonstrated impressive verbal skills, whether that meant getting your parents to let you stay up past your bedtime, persuading your dog to stop harassing the neighbors, or sweet-talking your spouse into forgiving you for yet again getting home late without calling.

We've all, at one time or another, savored the results of having said the right thing at the right time to the right person. We may have even been able to congratulate ourselves for having kept our mouths shut when it was appropriate but difficult. At least once or twice in our lives, we've responded to insults with a comeback either so funny or so gracious that it was worthy of Billy Crystal or Mother Teresa.

So, such responses are possible. With a little luck, they're even repeatable. The question is, Are such situations predictable? If they are, if they can be anticipated, then we can be trained and prepared to respond appropriately and effectively every time. Now there's a worthy goal.

Can we speak convincingly on those all-too-frequent days when we're overworked and exhausted? Can we expect the right words to tumble gracefully from our lips when we're negotiating a raise or trying to steer a child through negative peer pressure?

Do we know what to say when the plumber says he can't get to our faulty water heater for two days? Can we confront our spouse about a problem without irreparably damaging the marriage? Can we speak up at a staff meeting to make an unpopular but vital point without losing our fragile standing within the organization?

Do we know which words and inflections produce desired results? Have we any idea when to use them and when it's smarter to simply keep quiet?

And if we know these things, are we capable of using them when under pressure? Can we access them when situations turn ugly or potentially violent? Do we know what to say to keep a love relationship from sliding down the tubes?

Or is that when we're likely to take the cheapest shots, to make those statements that can never be taken back?

In short, can we get up in the morning and expect the right words to come out of our mouths that day, no matter what occurs? Or will we be taking our chances?

9

The Greatest Speech
You'll Ever Live
to Regret

WHEN WE EMPLOY the words that most naturally come to our lips, we run the risk of giving the greatest speech we'll ever live to regret. We wind up saying things we can never take back. This happens most often when we allow others to set the tone in confrontations.

We all deal with people "under the influence" nearly everyday. If it's not alcohol or drugs, it's frustration, fear, impatience, lack of self-worth, defensiveness, and a host of other influences. Doesn't it make sense that we should develop a state of mind that will allow us to skillfully interact with these people—whether they be criminals, customers, spouses, kids, or salesclerks—and not let them get our goats?

Nowhere in my long, formal education, did anyone train me in this. I was trained to confront people, to snap back at them to preserve my so-called identity. I had the macho notion that I wouldn't take any crap, any verbal abuse. Several years later I realized that being given abuse was something that would happen the rest of my life, so I'd better learn to handle it.

A HABIT OF MIND

A samurai warfare state of mind called *mushin* is defined as "the still center," or the ability to stay calm, read your opponent, and attempt to redirect his aggression in a more positive way. If you cannot keep a still center, you cannot stay in control of yourself or the situation.

The *mushin* state underlies both physical judo and Verbal Judo—a mind-mouth harmony, if you will. The English word closest to the idea of *mushin* is *disinterested*.

Many make the mistake of defining *disinterested* as uninterested. In fact, *disinterested* means impartial. *Dis* is from the Latin root meaning "not" and *interested* is from the Latin word meaning "biased." So the word means "not biased, open, flexible." As you can imagine, those are the three great traits of not only a good police officer, but also of any good communicator.

A closed mind misreads people and makes terrible errors. The flexible mind has the surviving strength of the willow tree, which survives even in heavy winds because it bends, it is malleable. This is precisely what we have to do and be when under the influence of verbal abuse.

Being malleable is always superior to that which is unmovable, thus the judo principle of controlling things by going along with them—mastery through adaptation. This allows you the strength to deal with people different from yourself.

I was never taught to deal with people who insulted me. I responded the natural, defensive way, which caused confrontation. I thought confrontation was the point. Now I know that a studied response of deflection and redirection is the answer. I discovered it in my study of ancient warfare. In an old samurai text, translated from the Japanese, an ancient master was quoted: "When man throws spear of insult at head, move head! Spear miss target, leave man empty-handed, spear in wall, not in you."

That was ten times better than the Western "sticks and stones may break my bones but names will never hurt me," because the latter isn't true. Insults wound deeply if we don't deflect them. Deflection is a nice concept, but how do you do it? (That's my complaint with most gurus—and samurai— they don't offer enough specificity. Fortunately, I found my answer in the streets.)

STRIP PHRASES

One night early in my career I stopped a pickup truck filled with angry, drunken cowboys after a rodeo. The driver, who appeared to be twice my size, was in my face, calling me all kinds of names. I asked to see his driver's license and he responded with a bunch of curses. Almost without thinking, I said, "Well, I 'preciate that, sir, but I need to see your license."

He kind of laughed me off but produced his license. Later it struck me that my colloquial use of the word *'preciate* was the key. Of course, it had been nonsense! He had impugned my ancestry and cast aspersions on my manhood, and I had said I appreciated it. Think about that. I was figuratively moving my head so his spear of insult clattered past me.

I used the abbreviated version of the word because, of course, I do *not* appreciate being called names. I could certainly *'preciate* where he was coming from, because I was emphathizing and trying to work with him. So I used *'preciate that* as what I now call a "strip phrase," a deflector that strips the insult of its power.

In the martial arts we teach people to deflect punches, but not hard, for if you block hard, you will push the antagonist away. That gives him more time to recover and possibly even pull a weapon. When a man throws a fist at your face, you want to move your face slightly at the very last instant allowing his fist to just graze the top of your head. Then you strike back because he's in close proximity.

My strip phrase deflector of the loudmouth cowboy was the same thing. Soon I developed other strip phrases, simple, shortened versions of calm answers. For instance, the next time a subject tried to humiliate me, I said, "I understan' that, sir, but listen to me: I need your driver's license." Again, to rationalize the absurdity of my statement in my own mind, I didn't use the whole, real word *understand*. I left the last letter off and that somehow allowed me to tell an idiot who had just called me every name in the book, "I understan' that."

Then I made up another one. It sounds like "oh yes," but I run it together as a one-word strip phrase, *oyesss*. I responded to every insult with *oyesss*. Soon I found that if I combined the strip phrases they worked even better. A guy would start in with, "You slimy, no-good blankety-blank of a—" and I would say, " 'Preciate that, oyesss, understan' that, sir, but let me see your license, please."

Crazy as it sounds, that works. I have heard some of the greatest communicators in the country use similar phrases, like "I hear ya, sir, but..." and "I got t'at, ma'am, but..." or "I b'lieve that, sir, but..." or "Tha'sa fact, but..."

These strip phrases deflect the insults coming at you and allow you to focus on what you're doing.

FOUR REASONS TO EMPLOY STRIP PHRASES

First, strip phrases actually make you feel good. Normally when you react in a pressure situation with phrases that make you feel good, you're probably doing no good. Because reacting to insults in a way that makes you feel good usually means you have reacted in kind. But, strip phrases make you feel legitimately good because you're being tactical and are responding—not reacting—to the problem, keeping your cool and remaining professional. When you *react,* you're being controlled by the situation. When you *respond,* you're dealing with it. (See Chapter 27 for a fuller explanation of the difference.)

When I worked in the Canine Unit the animal assigned to me was a police attack dog when his collar was on, and a family pet when that collar came off. Mama and the kids could roll around with that dog as long as his collar was off. The moment you put his collar on he went back to work, and then nobody messed with him. I use strip phrases when I have my professional collar on, and I relax on my own time.

Second, deflectors serve as what I call a "springboard focus technique." Strip phrases springboard you over all the insults that might otherwise allow the other person (a speeder, subordinate, angry child, complaining customer) to defeat you. Once you have avoided the hurled insult, you have springboarded to the word *but*, which brings me to Thompson's Law of the Street, which can be applied everywhere: After the word *but*, use only words that serve your professional purpose.

"Understan' that, sir, *but* I need to see your driver's license."

"I 'preciate that, *but* I need to see some identification."

Everything after the *but* is designed to get the job done.

Third, if you can springboard past the insults and focus on the goal, you have disempowered the other person. Say you're a clerk and someone comes into your store and blames you for a shirt that fell apart. He insults you, calls you incompetent, and questions your heritage. Your first reaction might naturally be "Hold on here! Don't blame me! You're not going to get any satisfaction if you take that tone!"

But notice, if you ignore the insult and springboard over it with an apology, an "I 'preciate that," you have disempowered him. You're winning! And you're feeling good.

Fourth, when you use these tactical phrases, you sound good. It's not enough to *be* good. You've also got to sound good, or it's no good. Because you lose credibility with anyone who overhears it. Springboarding allows you to sound good under pressure.

Before I move into a couple of hints for dealing with difficult people, I should add that there are times when it is good *not* to use strip phrases. When you sense that the strip phrase might be a danger in itself, because the person is agitated that you're clearly deflecting and not dealing with the conflict at hand, skip the strip phrases and deal with the issues immediately.

TWO PRINCIPLES FOR DEALING WITH DIFFICULT PEOPLE

If you understand and agree with my four reasons for using strip phrases, feel free to develop your own. Consider them your ammunition, like arrows in a quiver. Keep them readily accessible so you can use them without thinking. They will allow you to keep two principles before you at all times when dealing with difficult people:

Principle number one: Let the person say what he wants as long as he does what you say. I tell even cops that. I say, "Let them chip at you as long as they're cooperating with you. What do you care what they say? Your attitude should be 'Say what you want, but do as I say!' "

The only time this would not work is when the words the citizen uses serve only to inflate him with adrenaline, making him or his companions more of a problem. The officer has to carefully watch a person's body language to see when he might explode from his own initiative. It's important to intervene before these situations get out of hand.

In a business setting, remember that insulting people don't mean what they're saying anyway, so what do you care what they say? They are upset. Focus on their behavior, not on their attitude. As long as they are doing what you need them to do, let their mood blow over.

Principle number two: Always go for the win/win solution. I tell cops, "Look, you can give the citizen the last word because you have the last action." Let the perpetrator talk all he wants. You have the authority and the power to arrest him if necessary. If the civilian wants to shoot off his mouth to save face in front of his friends or family, that doesn't hurt you. Most of the verbal abuse cops get tends to be like the ink of a squid. It lets people hide, sounding good even if they're not looking good.

If you both take away people's last word *and* have the last act, you create violent scenarios and make enemies. Let 'em spout off. They win, you win.

A MOST IMPORTANT DISTINCTION

Another critical distinction I make for police officers, which everyone ought to know, is the difference between the word *REspect* and the word *respect*. REspect is what we have to show all people at all times. We cannot *respect* people who prey on others, people who beat their spouses, people who brutalize their children. I have no *respect* for lawbreakers, but when as a professional I deal with them, I must always show them *REspect*. That is the Golden Rule in a single word.

I know that is a difficult and fine line to draw because the words are spelled the same, sound nearly the same (except for the emphasis on different syllables), and seem to mean the same. But think of it this way: *RE* in Latin means to give back, as in giving back what you want under identical conditions. So, always treat the other person as you would want to be treated under identical conditions, even if he is not worthy of your respect. In other words, even in the process of arresting you, or firing you, or disciplining you, I must extend to you the kind of behavior I would expect were I in your shoes.

When we disrespect people, put them down in front of others, or make them feel bad, we lose our power and create more enemies. We lose our professional face. We get upset, we use language irresponsibly, and we no longer have a disinterested state of mind. We're no longer great warriors of words; we've become part of the problem.

If you can learn to deal skillfully with people under pressure, you can dance where others stumble. And that is the hallmark of the communication samurai: REspect to all, with dignity, pride, and assertiveness.

10

The Only Way
to Interrupt People
and Still Have Them
Love You

ONE OF THE most powerful verbal tools I know is Paraphrasing.

To paraphrase, put most simply, is to put another person's meaning into your words and deliver it back to him. If you're taking abuse, you want to somehow intrude so you can make the diatribe a conversation. Then you can cast what you think lies behind his aggressive words (his real point) in your own words (which will be calmer because you're not the emotionally charged one here), and be sure that you have heard it correctly.

When you paraphrase like that, you have actually inserted yet a third person into a two-person dialogue. Suddenly you have not his words with his meaning or your words with your meaning, but your words with his meaning. I'll get into the fourteen reasons why this is so effective, but first, how do you do this? There are two basic steps.

THE SWORD OF INSERTION

This weapon is that single sentence that allows you to cut into a tirade and take control. It's hard to stop people talking. They are upset and they can't be told "Get to the point!" All that will get you is "I *am* getting to the point! You're not listening." And don't tell people to shut up or to calm down or to let you talk, because they won't shut up, they won't calm down, and they won't let you talk.

So you start with the Sword of Insertion, a wedge into the harangue like "Whoa!" or "Listen!" (spoken earnestly, not in anger) or "Wait a second."

THE ULTIMATE EMPATHETIC SENTENCE

Here then is the powerful sentence that will allow you to interrupt anyone without fear of bodily harm: "Let me be sure I heard what you just said."

This simple sentence is so empathetic, so full of conciliation and cooperation, so pregnant with sincerity, that you'll hardly ever see someone let it slide by. What you're saying, in essence, is "Let me be sure I understand you. Let me be sure we're on the same wavelength. Let me be sure I heard that."

You have become the personification of empathy. Everything about that sentence says you're trying to understand. No matter how upset, just about anyone will shut up and listen because she too wants to be sure you heard what she said. In fact, the surer she is that you were *not* listening, the more likely she is to now hear you out, if only to prove you wrong!

FOURTEEN BENEFITS OF PARAPHRASING

One. Magically, in one sentence, by paraphrasing you've hooked the other person. He's listening. Using the Sword of

Insertion with that sentence is the only way I know to interrupt somebody without generating further resistance.

Two. You have taken control because you're talking and he is listening.

Three. You're making sure of what you heard right on the spot, not finding out later you misunderstood.

Four. If you have *not* heard the person accurately, he can correct you. That fills your pockets with ammunition. The more you know about somebody, the better, and the more he speaks, the more he reveals about his emotions, his prejudices, and his assumptions. That can only help you in deflecting insults, keeping his attention, and generating voluntary compliance.

Five. You have made the other person a better listener, because no one listens harder than he does to his own point of view. You're telling him, "Here's what I hear you saying," and you can bet he wants to hear that.

Six. You've created empathy. The other person will believe you're trying to understand. Whether you really are interested is irrelevant. What's important is that he thinks that you are, and nothing makes him more certain than that Sword of Insertion sentence "Whoa! Let me be sure I heard what you just said."

Seven. Once you have thrust the Sword of Insertion and pronounced the ultimate empathetic sentence, you have gained attention. Then, to effect this seventh benefit of paraphrasing you want to immediately follow up with something like this: "Okay, you are feeling X because of Y, true?" The X equals an emotion, like anger or frustration, and the Y equals a reason. You don't even have to be right. You're guessing at this point. For instance, it might go like this: "Whoa! Listen, let me be sure I understand what you're saying. You're feeling angry because you believe I purposely undermined you in front of your colleagues yesterday at the meeting."

Now the person can correct either the emotion you used for X or the reason you used for Y. He might say, "Well, no, I'm not angry. I'm disappointed." Now you're getting somewhere. Whether he's angry or disappointed will make a difference in where you go from there. Or he might modify X, the reason. "Yeah, I'm angry, but I'm not saying you purposely did it."

Notice that my being right is not the issue. Making the attempt to get it right is the issue, because I'm appearing concerned and it allows the upset person to modify his original statements. And that's the seventh benefit of paraphrasing. He's becoming more reasonable, without your having to vainly shout "Be reasonable!" (which never works).

Eight. Paraphrasing overcomes a strange phenomenon I call "sonic intention." People often think they have said something because they heard themselves say it in their mind, or because they had so carefully rehearsed it. Have you ever argued with your spouse about what was said the night before? You say, "You never said that!" And he or she says, "Oh yes I did!" Those arguments go on and on. What do you learn from this? Bottom line: If people think they said something, they said it, and no amount of argument or evidence will change their minds.

My advice in a situation like that is to give in, because I've tried arguing and I always wound up sleeping in the pickup truck.

Nine. This advantage to using paraphrasing is that it has a clarifying effect for people standing around. When you're dealing with a difficult person in public, whether in a store or an office or on the street, you don't want to be overheard sounding badly. Remember the ancient principle: Look good, sound good, or no good. Paraphrasing is gentle. It tones down the volume and makes a diatribe a conversation. There should be no condemnation in the completely disinterested voice, the essence of effective paraphrasing. Paraphrasing should make me sound as if I'm trying to work on the problem, rather than react to the problem.

Ten. The tenth advantage of paraphrasing is that it prevents metaphrasing—which I define as putting words (especially inaccurate ones) into other people's mouths. Metaphrasing is a perversion of paraphrasing.

Too often we're so concerned about what people *ought* to be saying that we paraphrase them as *we* would have said it. That always insults and angers people.

Metaphrasing is useful under only one condition. If you're working as a dispatcher, working the emergency phones, often you have to take control of a verbal encounter and extract information quickly. You'll want to use Step 1 of paraphrasing, the Sword of Insertion, "Whoa! Whoa! Let me be sure I heard what you just said." But then, instead of paraphrasing, move right to metaphrasing. In short, the person never again gets into the encounter except to answer pertinent questions. You're guiding the conversation quickly: "There's somebody in the back of your house? Can you see him? Does he have a weapon? Is he moving? Clarify your address for me again. We have officers on the way. What is the man doing? Can he see you?"

From that point on, the person who might otherwise panic and become hysterical and of no help is giving you information. Though your approach may sound aggressive, it shows tremendous concern. It gives the comforting impression that you are helping, that you are in control. Frightened people usually calm down when they think their crisis is finally being handled by somebody who cares.

I once heard the story of a lady who lived on a street corner where traffic accidents were common. She learned over the years to deal forthrightly with people who were injured or scared. One day a particularly hellacious collision resulted in an old woman being trapped in a car and her son, a middle-aged man, running to the corner house in a panic. "I don't want my mama to die out there," he wailed.

The lady met him at the door with blankets and a bottle of water *and* information. "I have already called the paramedics and they're on their way," she said. "Keep your mother warm and calm until they get here."

I asked how she knew someone was trapped in a car. "Because he came running. As soon as I heard the collision, I called nine-one-one and grabbed the blankets and the bottle. I knew the first thing out of his mouth would be the nature of the trouble, and I could tell by his face that he was frantic. I figured if I seemed to have things under control and could convince him his loved one needed to be kept calm, he would have to calm down too."

In most other situations metaphrasing does not work well, and paraphrasing is preferable.

Eleven. You can ask for reverse paraphrasing to be sure the other person understands you. If you want to be a better supervisor, or ensure that your children understand you, ask that they paraphrase back to you what they take to be your meaning.

I've found that up to seven of ten people will misread a document and miss the point. More horrifying, eight of ten misunderstand most verbal exchanges. It's easy to talk, but it's hard to listen well. And when you ask someone, "Do you understand what I've just said?" very few people will admit they missed your point. The key is not to ask for a negative answer. Ask the person to tell you what you said, and you'll get an accurate reading how you've communicated. Remember, the responsibility for the understanding belongs to the speaker, not the listener. Your job is to get through.

Be careful not to condescend by implying that you just know the person will misunderstand. Rather, put the onus on yourself. Ask him to repeat it back to you for *your* benefit: "To be sure I said what I intended to say, would you give back what you understand the point of this discussion has been?" People will do that, and it safeguards you.

Twelve. You also safeguard yourself by paraphrasing back what your boss or your spouse or children say. It's possible your supervisor may not say exactly what he or she meant. If you don't get it right, are you going to win the argument later? You walk in with a report your boss asked for two weeks before and he hits you with "I told you I needed you in here at ten o'clock so I could have that for my meeting at eleven. This report's worthless now."

You know full well he never said ten o'clock, and you thought you were several hours early with it. Are you going to say, "You never said it had to be to you by ten"?

In the interest of truth, you might try that. But then he or she says, "I most certainly did, and that was the most important part of the assignment. What's the matter with you?" Argue that one, right or wrong, and you're liable to be arguing for the last time. Your only recourse at that point is to say, "I'm sorry. I must not have heard it." If you had paraphrased before you left the office the first time, your boss would have heard either that you missed the time dead-line or that he or she forgot to mention it. It would be clar-ified, and your hard work would eventually pay off.

Don't rely on others to always say what they mean, no matter what their position. Paraphrase it back. That makes you look good, and it ensures a top level of professional work. (Besides, bosses love to hear themselves quoted!)

Thirteen. Paraphrasing has an unusual psychological ad-vantage I call "generating the fair-play response." Whoever you're paraphrasing is almost psychologically forced to play by the same rules and paraphrase you. People will generally treat you the way you treat them. It's kind of the Golden Rule again, applied to communication: Treat others as you would want to be treated under identical circumstances. So if you use paraphrasing, if you work people skillfully, they're apt—even despite their intentions—to give you equal time.

Fourteen. Finally, when you paraphrase, it etches the facts in your mind. If you have to write a report or you're phoning information back to your boss about the facts of a meeting, the paraphrasing reinforces your own memory. Your report, written or oral, will be more concise and more accurate.

Because the amazing tool of paraphrasing provides these fourteen different benefits, you see why I call it the most powerful tool in communication.

11

Verbal Judo Versus Verbal Karate

AT THE RISK of oversimplifying, let me assert that there are really only two kinds of language: Verbal Judo and Verbal Karate. Judo, as I've pointed out, was developed as a sport of self-defense without the use of weapons. Karate is defined as a self-defense system characterized by sharp, quick blows delivered with the hands and feet.

Thus, to me, Verbal Karate is the lashing out, as if with the side of a calloused hand, when you snap at your spouse, your children, your employer, your employees, anyone. Whenever you use in a harmful, destructive way those words that rise readily to your lips, you have employed the easiest use of language: Verbal Karate.

In the professional realm, Verbal Karate is the unprofessional use of language, because you're using words to express your personal feelings. You are not connecting with your audience, and basically you're off target.

Physical karate is a fighting, striking, kicking, attacking offensive system. When that approach is transferred to oral communication, it's easy to do, but it doesn't work. After thirty-five years of using both physical karate and Verbal

87

Karate professionally, I can tell you the latter never once helped me. And I was an expert at it.

In fact, Verbal Karate burned more bridges, alienated more people, and lost more opportunities for me than anything else I can think of. Oh, it often made me feel good about myself temporarily. I'd tell somebody off with my combination of educated articulation, physical prowess and presence, and macho tone of voice, and I'd strut away thinking, *I told him! You bet I did! He had it coming!*

A few hours later, without fail, I was thumping my forehead, thinking, *I should have said something else! Why did I say that? Why did I have to shoot off my big mouth?*

THE BAD NEWS

Of course, I usually had to go back and do some apologizing. The bad news is, there is no apology for verbal abuse. The best you can hope for is a shortened version of the word, like *'pologize* (much as I use with my strip phrases), because there is simply no taking back harmful words. You can say you take them back, but ask a person a decade later if he remembers your unkind words. Chances are, he will.

People never forget verbal abuse. It sinks deeper and festers longer than any other kind of abuse. I'd rather be cut with a sword than with an insult from someone I care about. Think of the times in your childhood you were humiliated by teachers or colleagues or peers. Have you forgotten them? That's why we must learn to use language more skillfully. That's why we must eschew Verbal Karate and embrace Verbal Judo.

THE GENTLE WAY

Physical judo was invented by a Dr. Kano in 1882. It was a derivative of jujitsu, which means "pain." Judo, as I mentioned in Chapter 4, means the gentle way, rather than the painful way. If you've ever seen a judo match, you may wonder what's gentle about it. People are thrown or foot-swept to the mat. The gentleness lies in the technique. You are not counteracting their approach and hammering back at them. Rather, you are moving with them, using their momentum to pull them off-balance and then propelling them to the ground. The way you throw someone allows him to break the fall and roll out of it. Verbal Judo, then, should be nonhurtful. It should be redirective rather than confrontational.

KELLEY AND THE CAR

All martial arts are based on redirection. I learned the concept of redirection when I first tried to put together a course in oral communication. I had been divorced (primarily because I didn't know how to use language and I'd snapped one too many times at my former spouse), and my then-sixteen-year-old daughter Kelley came to live with me in Albuquerque (apparently she was having trouble using words at home too).

A few weeks after moving in with me, Kelley came to me with a request. "Dad, I'm working part-time and I'm going to high school, and I gotta have a car."

Well, I was trying to start a business, and I was broke. I was living in a little condo and trying to keep up with the bills, so frankly Kelley's request, as legitimate as it may have been, made me mad. How presumptuous! What an ingrate! I wanted to say, "That's outrageous! What a request! How can you be so irrational as to think I have the money for that right now?" Those words welled up, but maybe I had learned enough about snapping at loved ones that I was able to control myself.

Instead, because I was working on these principles, I said, "Well now, Kelley, if I were to buy you a car, you would, of course, maintain it completely, true?"

"Oh yes, Dad. Oh yes."

I said, "Why don't you go check out what that means, and then let's talk."

Frankly, all I was doing was putting her off. I just needed her out of my hair, because otherwise I was not about to handle myself well.

A couple of days later she said, "Dad, buy me a bicycle."

I said, "What? What happened to the car?"

She said, "Are you kidding? Do you have any idea what maintenance and insurance would cost me? And then there's licensing and processing fees, to say nothing of gas and oil. I can't afford a car. Why don't you buy me a bike?"

I thought, *Great, George! You just saved thousands!*

But she continued, "You know, Dad, I notice you're beginning to travel, leaving your car at the airport and paying for parking. It must be lonely going to the airport and arriving home late at night, no one to meet you. It's not good for your car to be out there for days in cold weather. So, why don't you buy me a bike, and while you're in town, I ride bike, you drive car. But I will arrange my social life so I can take you to the airport on time and pick you up on time, making it easier for you. That way I can drive the car while you're away and you drive it when you're here."

Of course Kelley's was a great plan and worked out well. Without realizing it, I had redirected her attention and I avoided getting upset and starting a confrontation which could've lasted for weeks. Confrontation wouldn't have worked. Redirection did, and freed her to be more creative than I would have been. Verbal Judo had come to life for the very one who had discovered and hoped to promote it. Without realizing it, Kelley had actually employed Verbal Judo on me.

MASTERY THROUGH ADAPTING

Verbal Judo is simply the use of words to achieve your objective. You've got to stay in contact with your audience and use your words with maximum effectiveness and minimum effort. Why stir people up? There is a kind of mastery available through adapting. I didn't reject Kelley's request. I let it drift and refocused her attention until she became creative. I was becoming aware that Verbal Judo was the martial arts of the mind and the mouth, the ability to keep calm inside, to read the audience and find the right words for the right person at the right time.

Aristotle said that audiences are made, not found. You can trip over people who are angry and hostile, but if you're skillful, you can calm and redirect their behavior in two minutes.

FORCE OPTIONS

The goal of persuasion is to generate voluntary compliance. You can't expect it just because you play a certain authority role. You must make it happen. The great communicators have that art. They somehow get people to do what they want them to do by getting them to want to do it.

What force options are available to generating voluntary compliance? The first, surprisingly enough, is your mere presence: the way you show up, the way you approach, carry yourself, stand around, even the way you project your feelings onto your face. I teach police officers and corporate people the importance of professional presence, how they look as they enter a scene.

Consider, for example, a typical mistake: using the wrong facial expression—often with the wrong words. Many think they are going to cool people down and take charge of a situation by showing an angry, eyes-squinted-up, snarling face. That calms nobody down. If you want to calm somebody, don't you think it would be more helpful to affect a calm, pleasant, interested look?

HOW MANY FACES?

You have to have one face to calm somebody, another face to look interested, another to look concerned, and another when someone's trying to intimidate you. We all wear dozens of faces everyday. Which you use when will determine how successful you are in generating voluntary compliance, the goal of persuasion and an underlying tenet of Verbal Judo.

The Mount Rushmore frozen service face is the kind you run in to too often in businesses, government offices, or even hospitals. People just don't look happy. How about in retail stores where clerks wear Smile buttons but look thunderous? Those face are inappropriate.

Learn the skill of the chameleon, an image I have mounted on a pin and give out at my seminars. The chameleon is a good representation of an effective communicator because of its ability to adapt to its environment. Just as the chameleon changes colors to blend in, you must wear faces appropriate to changing situations. The chameleon survives because it adapts. No matter how you feel inside, you must develop the ability to look good on the outside—to reinforce what you're saying with a face and a demeanor that fits the situation.

This is hardly taught anywhere. When I ask police officers across the country to name their first force option, they usually tell me verbalization. Not true. It is professional presence, to look good. You've got to look the part.

Force option number two is verbalization: the right words for the right person at the right time. As Napoleon said, "More powerful than a standing army is the well-wrought word." Most of us do not communicate skillfully under pressure, yet our entire careers depend on it. I've already covered why "Calm down!" doesn't calm anybody down. Why not use a phrase like "It's gonna be all right. I'm working on it."

If people in crisis would remember these first two overriding force options, they would go a long way in improving communication. Without any other training or skill, they'll be on the right track by using the right words and having the right demeanor.

FOUR MORE FORCE OPTIONS

If words fail, and at times they do, go then to force option three: laying hands on a person and using techniques from the martial arts called the come-along holds. Obviously, these are limited to law enforcement personnel, and they help generate voluntary compliance at the lowest level of pain possible.

Option number four is the use of artificial incapacitators—chemical mace, stun guns, the kind of force that temporarily immobilizes so the police officer can generate voluntary compliance.

The fifth option, using impact tools like the nightstick or the baton, is not designed to permanently injure or brutalize people. These impact tools are to be used to generate voluntary compliance at a higher level of pain than the others—but only when necessary.

Option number six is deadly force, and, of course, that has nothing to do with generating voluntary compliance. Deadly force is used for enforced compliance, and there are strict rules—such as imminent jeopardy and preclusion (meaning no other force options are available)—that tell us when such extreme measures are allowed. Obviously, for most people the force options are much more limited.

YOUR OPTIONS

In corporate America or at home, it's important that you know the next force option after words fail. Since you can't cuff someone or subdue him with a stick or draw down on him—much as you would like to occasionally (be honest!)

it is crucial that your next move has some teeth in it. Is it a written warning, some kind of a transfer, a loss of money or privilege? One of the secrets of being a good communicator is knowing the system. Be sure you are well versed in policy. Too many people use threats they don't have the power to carry out. How about the mother who tells a toddler—near midnight at a family Christmas bash she had no business subjecting him to—"If you don't behave I'll put you out in the car"? Right.

Know what you can enforce and at what level you can enforce it. That gives you confidence and credibility. Credibility, which is rooted in the Latin word *credo*, meaning "I believe," begins and ends with your use of words.

The birth of my ability to communicate came in my acceptance of the fact that I was the problem. If you can accept that the problem with your spouse, your children, or at your workplace may be in your mirror, you can make dramatic changes in your ability to be skillful under pressure. Focus on technique, focus on the goal. Your ability to survive professionally and domestically lies with your ability to use words skillfully, and sometimes that means moving to tougher force options. While you don't have the tools of the police officer, or (I hope) the need for them, there is a system to handle the tougher-than-usual encounters.

12

The Five-Step
Hard Style

OVER NEARLY THE last two decades, I have taught Verbal
Judo to almost seventy thousand cops in nearly seven
hundred police departments, and to thousands more in corporate and retail America. When I teach, I also learn, and
if there's one thing I've learned from all these frontline communicators, it's this: If someone wants to ruin your credibility
and get the advantage over you, all he has to do is make you
angry enough to misuse words.

I believe that more than 90 percent of your success will
lie in your delivery style, so I want to provide you with a
series of principles to live by and to enact on a daily basis,
making you more effective as a parent, a professional, and
a friend.

DISCOVERED THE HARD WAY

Persuasion—generating voluntary compliance—is the essence of Verbal Judo, and at the heart of persuasion is a five-
step model .I discovered the hard way in police work. II

suggests that you (1) Ask (Ethical Appeal), (2) Set Context (Reasonable Appeal), (3) Present Options (Personal Appeal), (4) Confirm (Practical Appeal), and (5) Act (Determination of Appropriate Action). (For a full discussion of the four types of appeals, see Chapter 21.)

Obviously, this didn't all come to me in a flash. Less than a week after I got in trouble with the police chief over my brusque manner with citizens—remember in Chapter 3 all that hassling with offenders—I stopped another guy at about 3:00 A.M. He had ignored several stop signs, and when I approached his car I saw a whiskey bottle on the floor.

I snapped, "You, sir, step out!"

When I got the familiar response, "I'm not gettin' out of this car!" I thought, *Oh no. Here we go again.* I didn't want another tongue lashing from the chief, so I thought quickly and came at him from a slightly different direction. Let me remind you, I didn't know what I was doing was right. I was just scrambling to try to stay out of trouble and still get my job done.

I softened my tone and said, "Sir, listen to me. There's a whiskey bottle by your right leg. Now, sir, that constitutes under the law what we call an open-bottle charge. I have no choice but to have you step out, because I'm required to enter your vehicle and take a look at that bottle. For your safety and mine, sir, department policy says I have to ask you to step out. Would you do that for me?"

Make no mistake, I felt like a wimp at first. What I really wanted to do was pin the guy to the ground, cuff him up and rough him up and let him know he was tangling with the wrong lawman. You bet I did. But I was not going to let this guy get my goat, or my job. My calmer voice showed I was more in control. I switched from commanding to asking, and then I set the context by telling him why I was making my request.

The word *context* is crucial in all communication. *Context* comes from the Latin *contexo* (*contextus*) or possibly the Latin *con* and *texo.* Both mean "weave together" or "join." I have come to learn that of ten drivers who are Difficult People (see Chapter 5) and refuse to get out of the car at first request, at least seven will do what you say if you only tell them why. One of the great psychological urges in this country is the desire to know. If you can tap in to that and let people know why you're saying what you're saying, you can usually generate voluntary compliance. Give them context. Weave together the elements of the situation.

When I set context, I grounded myself in professionalism. I gave reasons, policies, and procedures for what I was asking. My ego, so prevalent in that first command, "Get Out!" was then missing. (Your personal face will always create conflict because you virtually force the public, especially the Difficult People, who are wired that way, to come back at you.) Hardly realizing it, I had substituted my professional face for my personal face. I had moved from the ethical appeal of asking to a reasonable appeal of setting context.

Unfortunately, I had run into one of the few Difficult People not motivated by having the request put into context. This guy required my going to Step 3, presenting options and making a personal appeal, because he said, "I don't know nothing about that bottle, Jack! I took a bunch of guys to a party last night and they drank whiskey. I don't even drink whiskey. Not my bottle, not my problem. I'm not gettin' out."

I gotta tell you, George Thompson the civilian would just as soon have run his nightstick through one of the guy's ears and out the other. But I'm a practical man. I like strokes as much as the next guy, and I didn't want my chief on my case again. I tried a new approach, coming at the driver from yet another direction.

I said, "Sir, listen, that's an interesting distinction between whether it's your bottle or your buddies', but the law does not make that distinction. The law says, 'Bottle in car, you driver, you responsible.' Now, sir, that might not even be fair, but 'tis so under the law. I'd like to think you'd cooperate with me. Step on out, sir. I can check that bottle, then I can chat with you about why I stopped you in the first place. That way it looks as if you're gonna be able to go home tonight, put your feet up, be with your family, eat at your own table, sleep in your own bed, and get up in the morning and go to work. I'd like to think you'd want to do that, sir, but the law gives you another option if you wish. The law says if you want, you can come with us, eat with us, stay overnight, sleep with us. That's called an arrest. Now, I don't see any need to do that. That's a lot of paperwork for me, that's towing your car, and you know they'll put dents on that thing down at the yard. You don't need that kind of trouble, do you, sir? Why don't you give us both a break and cooperate with me and step on out of there?"

Those were options, not threats, and they worked. Basically all I told the guy was he could get out of the car or go to jail, but notice that I left the power of choice with him. Notice also how specific I was. Specificity is one of the secrets of persuasion—helping people see what you want them to see. I tried to paint a picture of his going home, the problem over, contrasted with a picture of his coming with me, having his car towed, and going to jail. Those specifics made his choice clear and easy.

I knew I'd hit on something when the guy laughed and said, "I don't need that kind of trouble, Officer," and stepped out. Best of all, and here's the point, he lost no face and he stepped out onto ground that I had created for him.

THE WHAT-IFS?

What if he hadn't stepped out? Or what if your adversary still doesn't cooperate when you've reach the third step of the Five-Step Hard Style? Unless you're a cop, you may have met your match. Just for the sake of illustration, let me tell you what police officers sometimes have to do. They must move to what I call practical appeal, which is to confirm the resistance. Until my course began reaching police departments across America, cops really had no option at that point but to haul people out of their cars, using come-along holds. My contention is that there is one optional sentence left that still gives a troublemaker a chance to do the right thing and save further hassle.

If he hasn't pulled a weapon, there's a powerful sentence worth trying—and one you can use with your children, co-workers, or troublesome customers. It's this: "Is there anything I can say or do at this time to earn your cooperation?" And then I always follow it with the optimistic "I'd sure like to think there is."

Notice how pleasant and positive that is. I've seen this work on the street in tough cities in California and in Seattle, Washington. I saw this work with a guy who had fought the cops seventeen straight times before an officer tried this fourth step, the confirmation, which confirms whether or not the person will cooperate.

If this doesn't work, and very occasionally it doesn't, then the officer must act—Step 5. Interestingly for cops working in pairs is that the practical appeal question tips off the partner that Step 5 is next. If the perpetrator makes it clear that there is nothing that can be said or done to gain his cooperation, it's time for action. I have alerted my partner, who is then moving to the next position, without having warned the subject.

The wrong language in that situation, the "if you don't do this I'm going to do that" approach, always warns people that we're about to act, making them dangerously ready for us. If I say to a subject, "Get out or I'm going to take you out!" he may come at me with a razor blade. But my suggested sentence is so pleasant that it keeps him off-balance. It allows me to justify my action later in court and sound good, and it alerts my partner without alerting the perpetrator. Now if the guy says, "That's right, I'm not getting out," the cop takes him out before he finishes the next sentence.

USING THIS AT HOME

Most of us have not been trained to deal with teenagers. Up to about age eleven or twelve, kids may give us some trouble, but basically they follow our directions. By the time they get to be thirteen or so, they enter the Why Generation. Everything that was once accepted is now questioned. I don't know about you, but that's where I found myself less effective than ever as a parent. No one ever told me how to persuade a teenager, but now I know that the Five-Step Hard Style is the key to persuasion.

For example, suppose I were to tell my son, "Taylor, before you go to the party, take the trash out."

I might hear something like "Hey, Dad, I haven't got time to do it tonight. I'm in a rush. Why don't you do it?" *Why don't I do it?* Most of us would snap at that response. We don't set context or lay out options. We just move right to Step 3 and turn options into threats: "Hey, you don't take the trash out, you don't go out!"

Of course, all that gets you from the teenager is "That's unfair, I have to do everything, you never do anything, blah, blah, blah." Suddenly you've got yourself serious argument.

Why not pleasantly go to Step 2—setting context? "Taylor, remember when we agreed six months ago that your allowance would be partially based on getting that trash to the curb every Friday night, before going out? Why don't you just keep your word and do it?"

For some kids, appealing to their honor works immediately, as it usually does with my son. But what if you have a difficult teenager? You're apt to hear, "Yeah, well, I meant to talk to you about that allowance business, anyway. I'm fed up with that. Get someone else to take the trash out because I'm in a hurry."

Now it's time to go to setting and creating options instead of threats. Something like this might work: "Taylor, listen, we agreed, 'When cans by curb, Taylor out for parties.' You don't have to physically take them out; your job is to see that they get out. If you want to bribe your sister or get Mama to take them out or you want to use voodoo, I don't care. No cans out, no party."

At this point, most kids would probably do it. There's been no assault on Taylor's personal face, and he can maintain his dignity by simply taking the trash out. But suppose he doesn't. Suppose he says, "I'm not gonna do it! I'm in a hurry!" Then you have no choice. You move right to Step 4. "Taylor, listen! Is there anything I can say or do at this time to earn your cooperation and get you to keep your word and take the trash out? I'd sure like to think there is."

I don't know about your kids, but most kids know by that sentence that discussion is about over. The teenager can still take out the trash at that point and lose no credibility, no personal face. If he doesn't, you can ground him, send him to his room, take away his allowance, or whatever punishment is appropriate in your house. But notice that he cannot blame you. In the end it was his choice. The punishment is an appropriate action based on a fourth step that he resisted. He had a right to resist. That's how he earns his identity over time, flexing his muscles. We have to give our kids room to flex. If we're always coming down on them, they can't grow. But they must pay the consequences if they do not obey. Once the line is drawn, they must not cross it without punishment. Up to that point, we owe them the courtesy of looking for the keys to voluntary compliance.

The Five-Step Hard Style is a communication tactic that arms you to deal with difficult people under almost any condition. It provides you with decisiveness and certainty. You will always know where you are. You are in the asking stage (Step 1), the setting the context (telling why) stage (Step 2), the presenting of options (in the other person's best interest) stage (Step 3), or the confirming (that some kind of cooperation is either forthcoming or not) stage (Step 4). If not, you have to act (Step 5).

You will never again be trapped into repeating orders over and over, which is a great sign of weakness in a parent, a police officer, an executive, or anyone in a position of authority. Repetition reveals weakness. Flexibility and variance of approach shows strength.

13

The First Great Communication Art: Representation

YOUR PRESENCE AND your words, when skillfully combined, are knowledge and power in action. They allow you to generate voluntary compliance from the most difficult subjects. Now let me suggest that if you deal with people in any profession you have an identity that can be very clearly defined, one in which you can take great pride. You can be a Contact Professional.

Contact is an interesting word from the Latin *con* meaning "with" and *tact* meaning "to touch on all sides." I always emphasize the necessity of being a pro rather than an amateur. Amateurs have good days and bad days. They have not been trained to be tactical.

A professional, for example, is someone like Michael Jordan. He plays the greatest basketball in the world game after game but what really sets him apart is what he does under pressure. What does he do when you double-team him? I'll tell you what he does. He gets better. He passes more often, he passes better, he scores more, he has more assists.

You should take pride in your ability to get better under the pressure people put on you in the workplace. To be a contact professional who can handle any kind of stress, you must exude credibility and an aura of power.

In all the fancy courses I took and all the degrees I earned, I never had a course on how to handle my own weaknesses in interpersonal relationships. I learned this through experience and dealing with people. I learned that to be a contact professional you must first, of course, be in contact with yourself. Most of us have weaknesses in dealing with people. What are yours? Is there a list of five or six things that get under your skin about difficult people?

We all have buttons and triggers, but if you're going to work for others and represent them, you must not allow people to push your button or pull your trigger. The question is, how do you build a trigger guard? The answer: Know thyself. The old samurai used to say that if you don't know yourself, you lose 100 percent of the time.

THE "WANNA BET?" GUY

I discovered very early on as a police officer that one thing I hated was having my authority challenged. There was always somebody who'd say in a nasty, whiny, contentious voice, "You can't do that to me!" It seems I heard that twenty or thirty times a day, and it always angered me. Every time, a little voice went off in my head, *You wanna bet? Watch me!* Immediately I would take a more aggressive, attacking stance, and each time I made errors I was not able to explain them on paper or justify them to a superior.

The only person who had ever said anything about that problem was the old Indian who taught me things while I was growing up. One day when I was eleven, he said out of the blue, "Thompson, some day you will have enemies. Here's how you handle 'em. First always define. Then, name them. Then you will own them." The Indian walked off

into the forest and I thought, *What? What does that mean?*
It sounded kind of like some Indian folklore, and I hardly
gave it another thought until I was thirty-five. Then I was
on the streets, making enemies and not being able to handle
them.

I still didn't understand his advice, but I acted on it
anyway. What did I have to lose? I knew my biggest enemy
was anyone who challenged my authority. One day I wrote
that down. I had defined him. Naming him was more difficult, but I finally decided to call him by the voice that went
off inside of me. That voice always said, "Wanna bet?" So I
called my enemy the "Wanna Bet?" Guy. I said to myself,
"George, be careful of the 'Wanna Bet?' Guy or he'll own
you somewhere, sometime."

The very next night I placed a young man under arrest,
and he came back with "You can't touch me. I'll do what I
want. My father's on the city council; he'll have your job!"

Immediately I thought, *Wanna bet?* But at the same time,
a warning bell also went off in my head. *There he is, the "Wanna
Bet?" Guy! Be careful! He's gonna get you!*

I literally took a step back, forcing myself to remain calm
and not say or do anything that would jeopardize the integrity
of that very legitimate arrest. I wanted the bust, all right, and
I wanted it to stick because of the kid's snotty attitude. I could
have lost it all—and maybe even my job—if I had let him get
to me and make me do something stupid. I didn't, and *he*
got in big trouble.

To this day you cannot challenge my authority and make
me show anger. Sure, I'm still angry inside. My trigger has
been cocked, but you can't pull it. My trigger guard is in
place. I defined my enemy, and I named him. Now I own
him, rather than the other way around. What is your enemy?
Define it. Name it. Own it.

THE TEDDY BEAR TRUTH

I remained so intrigued by the power of that truth that about ten years later I asked a psychologist why it worked. He told me that when we define our weaknesses, or our so-called communication enemies, we actually bring them out and make them part of our consciousness. We admit them, bringing them into the light of recognition. We can name only that which we own, so when we name them, we acknowledge that we have taken ownership of them.

If you've ever taken your child to a store and bought him a teddy bear from a whole group of similar-looking bears, you know that by the time you've gotten to the counter, your child has named the bear. And if that teddy bear is ever misplaced or missing, you see your child bereft and heartbroken because by naming it, he has made it part of who he is. (For this reason farmers don't allow their children to name the heifers or the chickens. You can't very well serve up Elsie or Tweety Bird on a plate.)

Make a list of your most harmful weaknesses. Then name them. Give each a little tag and pin it wriggling to the wall of definition. Then you own them. Once you're in control inside, you can be in control outside. As a contact professional, you work in a highly visible world. You live and speak in a fishbowl. Every time you speak people are watching you. There are a lot of eyes out there, so you have to be careful. Say only what you'd be proud to have quoted back to you on Monday morning. And that all starts with knowing and being in contact with yourself.

REPRESENTATION

To be a top-flight contact professional, you have to become an artist at representation, the first of three great communication arts. Besides being in contact with (or knowing) yourself, you must be in contact with your organization and its constituency. As you do your professional representation work, you stand between the proverbial rock and hard place.

Just for fun, sketch out an illustration that will make this clearer. Draw a circle with the name of whatever organization or company you represent in it. To the right of that, draw a five-point star to represent you. To the right of that, draw a box with a *C* in it, which stands for your contact point (your constituency or customer or public). Every time you speak you represent everything in the circle on the left (the rock) to the contact in the square on the right (the hard place).

Now draw a figure eight, which represents your job, that begins on the left, passes through you, and continues to the right before coming back through you again. Continue to trace that figure eight, which signifies how you serve as a conduit between the two other entities *in such a manner as to generate voluntary compliance.*

I emphasize that because it means you are continually serving as a conduit. Keep tracing that figure eight and soon you'll see that you, the star, are virtually obliterated by your representational job. Now draw an arrow between the circle and the square and you have a figure eight with an arrow driven through the middle. That is the essence of representation: the ability to represent the spirit of your organization, its goods, its goals, its produce, its policies, its philosophy. It is that philosophy that you must fully know and embrace, because every time you open your mouth, you personify it to whomever you're talking to.

If you do your job right, as I hope you drew your illustration, you've disappeared. And that's one of my crucial points. When you speak, you are a mouthpiece, a representative. You do not represent your own ego. Remember, the more ego you show, the less power you have over people. Egotists only create conflict. The great communicators put their egos behind them and put the purpose and goal of communication before them. Nobody likes people whose personalities intrude.

If you're in a retail business, your job is to represent your organization in such a way as to not only get customers to buy the first time, but also to ensure they'll want to come back again and again. Nordstrom's was the first of many companies that has learned this art. It gave people pride in the organization.

Every time you open your mouth, you represent the boss, whether that is the chief of police, the mayor, the company president or CEO, or whoever. You speak for him and for everyone else who works in the organization. If I as a police officer were to bad-mouth people on the street and make them feel bad, they would go away not thinking about George Thompson (they rarely get my name or badge number), but rather the department. Research shows that if someone has a bad experience with a police officer he will tell twenty-seven to twenty-eight people over the next three days. Imagine the statistics for bad experiences in stores or with companies. If someone in your organization treats people poorly, he lowers your credibility and the credibility of everyone you care about in the company—and he makes your job far more difficult.

Effective professional language is that which contributes to voluntary compliance. Any language that makes compliance more difficult should be shunned. It may make *you* feel good to insult somebody, to tell him what you really think. But remember, if it makes you feel good, most of the time it won't work, or as the samurai were fond of saying, "If it makes you feel good, no good."

UNDER THE INFLUENCE

Your customer or client or citizen is under various kinds of influence. He may be under the influence of anxiety, fear, misunderstanding, ignorance, rage, even liquor and drugs. You have to learn to read people carefully. The old samurai who said that if you don't know yourself, you lose 100 percent of the time, also said, "If you know yourself but you do not know the opponent, you'll be lucky to win fifty percent of the time. If you know yourself and you know the opponent, you can win a hundred percent of the time."

That means one of the greatest communication skills is listening, really listening to people—to what they say and how they say it. And that leads me to the second great communication art.

14

The Second Great Communication Art: Translation

Once you have mastered the art of representation, translation becomes crucial. Translation is the ability to put what you say in the most proper, fitting, assertive, and powerful words possible. The goal is to put the precise meaning in your mind into your listener's mind. That means doing whatever is necessary to avoid the misunderstanding that comes with normal distractions and influences.

In many ways, this is a simple process, communication boiled down to its four basic elements:

1. **Content.** You have to know what you're talking about. As a professional or a parent, you must decide precisely what it is you want and need to communicate.

2. **Coding.** Coding is merely putting your message into words. This involves thinking of those words as a code that reflects your meaning. Think, for example, how many ways there are to tell a man you cannot help him. Or to tell a man to step out of his car. How many ways there are to tell your spouse you are sorry—most not as effective as they could be. Words should be seen as a way of reflecting meaning, but not ego—

you must separate your words (meaning) from your self (ego).

3. **Sending.** Once you know your meaning and have chosen the words for it, it's time to transmit it, whether by phone or in person, using your voice and other nonverbals (facial expressions, body language, etc.).

4. **Decoding.** Decoding is the responsibility of the hearer, but how well he decodes is in direct proportion to the effectiveness of the content, coding, and sending—yours. His decoding is also affected by your demeanor and carriage (voice and body language), external noise (cars, planes, phones, people, etc.), and his own internal noise (what I call "brain damage," or any other influence he may be under).

Most of us suffer from some level of brain damage. We don't like to be told what to do, perhaps. Or we're tired or think we've done enough for one day and we're ready to misunderstand what others are about to say. No wonder it's a nightmare to communicate. What looks like a simple process is actually difficult. We certainly will never get through to each other if we use the words that rise most naturally to our lips. We must remember if we do, we may wind up giving the greatest speech we'll ever live to regret.

OF RABBITS AND GREEN CHEESE

Natural language is disastrous. That's what makes translation indispensable. I once heard a very interesting story that I believe proves my point:

Neil Armstrong, the U.S. astronaut who in 1969 was the first man to walk on the moon, went on a world tour in 1972. In Japan he was asked by a tiny grade school child what it was really like on the moon. When Armstrong heard the translation he must have thought it a pretty simple question. He could have written a book on the subject. Rather than get into a long, complex answer for his young, Japanese-speaking audience, he responded with a quick bit of humor. He said, "Well, I didn't find a man in the moon or any green cheese, that's for sure!"

The Japanese translator told the children that Mr. Armstrong had said, "Well, I didn't find any rabbits on the moon, that's for sure!"

Now was that a good translation or a bad one? Believe it or not, it was excellent. Japanese culture contains no stories about a man in the moon or the moon being made of green cheese. In a full moon, they see a huge, pregnant rabbit, rather than a man. I've always seen her. Many northeast Indians see the same thing, as do many other Asians. On the lower right side (at about 5 o'clock) of the moon they see a gray blotch they regard as a hutch of baby rabbits. They tell hundreds of stories to their children about the moon's Mama Rabbit and her babies.

You'll notice that though the words were different, the meaning was the same. Armstrong was saying, in effect, that when he got to the moon, it wasn't at all what it appears from Earth. In our culture that would mean no man and no green cheese. In Japanese culture it means no Mama Rabbit or baby rabbits.

Frankly, that kind of translating is what you do every day if you're communicating effectively. The police officer on the street has to figure out what kind of language will be most assertive and effective to calm a subject and redirect his behavior. What might work for the little old lady from Pasadena might not work for a young gentleman from Albuquerque. The language a cop would use for some country club yuppie would be totally different from what he might use for a gang member in Watts. He may be transmitting the same message, but you can be sure there will be entirely different words for widely differing people.

My rule is: Treat everyone the same (with REspect and dignity), but don't talk to everyone the same way. You don't talk to each of your children the same way, do you? Since each responds differently, based on his or her makeup and character, you instinctively learn to communicate uniquely to each one.

The great cops I've watched and worked with, the great salespeople I've watched and listened to, and the great teachers I've studied under all have the same art. They may not think about it or dissect it as I do, but they will tell you that knowing one's audience and communicating in his language is one of the greatest skills there is.

Some people are able to do this naturally, but still they have to figuratively stand in the other person's shoes. And that brings us back to empathy. If you're having trouble communicating with those from different walks of life, it may be because you're thinking about yourself instead of about them. If you allow your ego to get in the way, you will find yourself using your own language instead of the other person's.

The great salesperson listens to people and interacts with them awhile, then suddenly begins to use the right kinds of words, whether they be emotional or pictorial, to paint an effective picture. To effectively represent anyone or anything, you must get out of yourself and get into others. I've seen that taught nowhere else, yet it is a great fundamental skill. Get rid of your ego, put yourself into your job, and take pride that as a contact professional you can walk the walk and talk the talk of your corporation or your business, and that you care enough about whom you're dealing with to use the right words for the right person at the right time.

Before I get into the third great communication art, mediation, I want to cover some important information on the subject of listening, to help put all three of the arts in perspective. My goal is to give you the skills, the tactics, and the philosophies you need to maximize your power in representation, translation, and mediation, so you can take pride in your artistry.

AN UNNATURAL ACT

Listening is not a natural act. It is highly artificial and artistic. In fact, listening is *not* the opposite of talking, and if you think it is, you're as brain-damaged as I used to be. In our culture, the opposite of talking is more like waiting to interrupt.

Active listening is a highly complex skill that has four different steps: Being open and unbiased, hearing literally, interpreting the data, and acting.

Don't ever assume people are open and ready to listen. One thing that makes my course different from so many others is that I, having been on the streets, know that communication is not the listener's responsibility. It is the sender's. As a police officer I had to ensure that I made people more cooperative and willing to be voluntarily compliant.

High school teachers tell me, "I have a bad class. What can I do about that?"

I say, "There is no such thing as a bad class. Only bad teaching." Sorry, but the responsibility of getting through lies with the teacher. I almost always start out with difficult classes, because the attendees are usually mandated to be there. They don't think they want to be taught. They're already professionals. They're on the street, dealing in dangerous situations all day, and they're pretty sure that some Ph.D. won't be able to tell them anything new—especially about talking their way out of situations rather than taking charge physically. I have to perform in such a way as to get and hold their attention.

Take the responsibility to be a good communicator. Get people to listen by the power and manner with which you send your message.

When you're on the listening end, you may be open and unbiased and able to literally hear, but how do you interpret what you've heard so you can decide on a course of action? Start with one of my undeniable, inarguable, street-survival truths: People hardly ever say what they mean. If you react to what they say, you make a mistake. People under the influence of liquor, drugs, rage, fear, anxiety, ignorance, stupidity, or bias, don't mean anything they say.

If you begin to grasp this point, you can become a more effective communicator. Here are two examples.

Deputy on the Doorstep

I was going to teach Verbal Judo to a sheriff's department, so the night before the classes I went on a ride-along with a young deputy. He answered a burglary call and knocked on the door. Before the deputy could ask the nature of the problem, he was hit with "Where the heck have you people been? I called three and a half hours ago and you're just showing up now! This is a lot of crap! You know, I'm tired of you people. My taxes pay your salaries and you're never here when I need you! I'm sick of this. Look at my house! It's stripped, everything gone, and what are you doing? Drinking coffee, having doughnuts, fooling around! You people write parking tickets when you should be enforcing the law!" And that was just the beginning.

The deputy, of course, had had a tough day too, so he snapped off the words that came most naturally to his lips. "Hey, listen to me, sir, I don't have to listen to this. I'm not paid enough to take your verbal abuse. I'm here, so if you want some help, I'll give you some help. You want to stand there and rant and rave at me, I'm going to go back into service and let you handle your own problem." He turned to walk off the porch, and of course the guy hit the roof.

From what you've learned already, what should the deputy have said? All the words thrown at him were born of rage and frustration. The citizen, a victim, didn't mean a word of that diatribe. What he really meant were four different things:

1. "I need some help."
2. "Can I get any of my stuff back?"

3. "How can I keep this from happening again? It's a jungle out there."

4. "What do I do with the feeling of having just been raped?"

If you have ever been burglarized, you know how the victim felt. It is no minor event. Somebody has been in your house. Many people can't even live in their houses after an intrusion and violation like that.

Now, why didn't the citizen say those four things? Why did he resort to every cliché he'd ever heard about what cops are doing when they're not on the scene? Because he was upset. He was frustrated. He was going to take it out on somebody.

Now, how would the Michael Jordan of communication have responded? Someone who understood that the man had not meant what he said and knew where the real meaning lay would have used a Sword of Insertion and gone on from there. Something like "Sir, listen to me. Whoa, I 'preciate that! You're right, it's a jungle out there or I would've been here sooner. But I'm here now, sir, and here's what I need to do. I need to see where those people got in the house and where they got out. And you need to conduct me on that tour and assist me in that investigation.

"While you're doing that, sir, I want you to be thinking very carefully about what is missing. Do you have pictures, serial numbers, markings on the stuff stolen? Because when we're done, I'm going to sit down with you and do a police report. This doesn't have to be meaningless paperwork. With a good report and lots of specifics, our department is often able to return thirty-five to forty percent of stolen property over time, some of it in reusable condition. I'd like to think maybe that could happen for you.

"Before I leave, let me tell you another thing, sir. You rightly pointed out how busy I am, but I'm never too busy that I can't take a minute or two to walk you around your house before leaving and point out some ways that you can safeguard it. I'm an expert in that area. May I come in?"

I have to believe that would get a cop into just about any house in America. The citizen may still be smoking and sputtering, but the cop's job is getting done.

The deputy should have two goals. First, he needs to get in and get out quickly and professionally. The computer screen in his squad car is full of calls waiting for action. Second, and just as important, the deputy needs to leave the citizen feeling better about the deputy than he ever thought he would when he first opened that door. The caller should know and be able to say, "That officer cared."

The Hostage Situation

A man holding hostages once told me, "I want a million dollars and an airplane!"

I said, "So do I!" and I laughed. Humor, carefully used, can be a deflector, an identifying factor, a way to forge a bond and work with a dangerous personality. I went on, "Sir, we'd both like those things, wouldn't we? But let me tell you something I think you already know. That's not going to happen. The people surrounding the house, sir, they don't like you. They're the SWAT team, and they want to kill you. To be frank with you, that's not the police chief and command officers on the roofs over there. Those happen to be Vietnam veterans, and their only job is to come in here and take you out.

"Now look, I work for these people, and they don't even like me. Let's you and I work together and see if we can't come up with something that will put something in your pocket. Let's see what we can do about your drinking coffee tomorrow night and having your lady over for dinner. Those things I might be able to help you do. As it stands now, they're not going to let you do that, so give me something I can take back to them and I'll see what I can do about getting you out of here alive and not in such deep trouble."

He worked with me, because I hadn't reacted to his words. I calmed him by telling him the truth. He wasn't going to get a million dollars and an airplane any more than I was, but that didn't mean I couldn't address his needs. Hostage takers, just like children, express their demands and desires. We are not in the business of meeting those. Whether in our roles as cops or parents, we're in the business not of satisfying demands, but of meeting needs.

If you gave your children everything they wanted, you'd turn them into mean, nasty little yuppies. You'd be working two and three jobs, and you'd grow old quick and die. Never react to what people say. React to what they mean. Just remember: People hardly ever say what they mean.

15

The Third Great Communication Art: Mediation

In 1972 an interesting experiment was done by a school of communication in the east. They took a toddler, barely verbal, to a safe spot near a busy intersection and told him to watch the cars. He was fascinated by the motion of the traffic, and for as long as it held his attention, they let him watch.

Then he was asked, "What did you see?"

The little boy said, naïvely but accurately, "Sometimes cars go this way and sometimes they go that way. They stop here; they go there."

The little boy was told, "That's good. Now look up there." Without hearing any more explanation, the boy noticed the traffic light and soon began to see it change colors. Within twenty minutes he was able to recognize order out of what had appeared disorder and make sense of what had appeared nonsense. He said, "Red, stop. Green, go. Yellow, I don't know."

The point of that story for my purposes is that the person who pointed out the traffic light was a mediator. The great service of the mediator, whether it's a psychologist helping you and your spouse live in harmony or a police officer work ing with somebody who refuses to get out of a car, is to help people see something new.

Mediators do this by fulfilling one of the definitions of the Latin word *medius,* "one who goes between." Effective mediators go between or across your experience, enabling you to see something in a new way. In short, they educate, making sense out of things by putting them into perspective.

THE MOUNTAIN MAN IN THE ALLEY

It had never struck me in my thirty-five years prior to becoming a police officer that mediation was one of the great communication arts. But soon my training sergeant, Bruce Fair, began to teach me without knowing it. First there was his ability to "separate and suture" warring couples. He would get them apart, calm them, and bring them back together, usually without an arrest or a bunch of paperwork. Then, of course, came the night he mediated a domestic dispute by reading the paper and asking to use the phone of an arguing couple (see Chapter 1).

After my training period with Bruce, I had been out on my own for about two months when I got a call that a man had broken up some tables in a bar and had fled southbound into my beat. The man was described as about six feet seven inches and almost three hundred pounds, white, no shirt, sweating profusely, and known to be violent. Just what I needed on a one-officer beat.

Sure enough, about twenty minutes later I was sharking (cruising slowly back and forth) behind some taverns when I spotted the guy in an alley with only one outlet—past me. I immediately radioed for help. I said, "I've got a man here as big as a house!"

A civilian can roll up the windows, lock the doors, and drive off as if he's seen nothing. As a cop, I knew I had to deal with the man. I stepped out of the car maybe forty feet from him, planning to use words to stall him until my backups arrived. I'd never had a course in tactical communication.

The man was holding a broken, jagged whiskey bottle by its neck, and he began to move toward me. I took a deep breath and worked at not sounding as scared as I was. I said, "Sir, I understand you broke up some tables and left a bar without paying. The bartender's pressing charges. Disorderly conduct, destruction of private property, theft of services. Put the bottle down, sir, and come with me. You're under arrest."

Saying so doesn't make it so. The man mountain looked me up and down and said, "You ain't big enough to take me down. Look at you, you're just a little punk!" Meanwhile, he was slowly, drunkenly shuffling toward me.

Frankly, I thought he had a pretty good point, so I drew my stick and backed away a bit. Right then, without my realizing it until several years later, Verbal Judo was conceived. I said, "What are you going to do, sir, cut me with that bottle? Listen, you're a great big guy. You can beat me up, no problem. Look at this face. It's been hurt before. But let me tell you something. All I'm trying to arrest you for is disorderly conduct. That's just a misdemeanor. You'll be in jail overnight and then you're out. Cost you maybe thirty bucks if you're guilty. Then you're home.

"Takin' me down is not such a hot idea. You hear those sirens? They're coming for you, sir. Men with big sticks and dogs, people who like to fight. You may hurt some of them, but bottom line you're going to jail. Then you'll be looking at a felony. That's more like ninety days and hundreds of dollars in fines."

He was still coming, and I was still talking. "Do you have a job?"

"Yeah."

"Well, you won't when you get out. What about a woman? Have you got yourself a lady at home?"

"Yeah."

Fortunately I knew enough to say she *might* be there when he got out. If I'd outright predicted she would abandon him while he was in jail, he would have wanted to fight me on that basis alone.

"Listen," I said, "you can do what you want. But let me tell you that that bottle is constituting, as you hold it, a felony. Look, the bartender's charge is a misdemeanor. I'm looking for a misdemeanor, and you're trying to turn it into a felony. Why don't you give me a break and I'll cut you some slack. Let's say I didn't see the bottle. You drop it and come with me, and all we've got is a misdemeanor."

To my amazement, he looked at the bottle as if seeing it for the first time and tossed it aside. He stopped moving, so I said, "Turn around!" And, by gosh, he did! I said, "Put your hands behind you," and he did that too. I cuffed him up, put him in the car, and headed to the jail. As I pulled out of the alley, two backup patrol cars, filled with officers and dogs and sticks, pulled in with their lights flashing. Realizing I didn't need them, I felt a strange sense of power I'd never felt before. I was safe, my uniform wasn't ripped (which I would have had to pay for), my face was not bleeding, the other cars could go back into service for the community, and I would be back on patrol in ten minutes. I thought, *Boy, that's power!*

Later, as I debriefed with Bruce Fair, I got a handle on what had gone right in a situation that could have gone all wrong. Here was a man under the influence of liquor, rage, fear, and pride. If I had confronted him, as I had been trained to do, I would have been in for serious violence.

Instead, I had redirected his behavior by cutting across his experience (mediating) and giving him a fresh, personal view of the situation from his own perspective. In essence, making it up as I went along, I used five different pieces of bait to hook him. I got him to think of the value of his time (one night in jail versus several weeks), his money (thirty dollars versus hundreds), his job (working versus unemployment), his record (misdemeanor versus felony), and his woman (might be there versus might not).

You'll notice that the essence of mediation lies in what I call the personal appeal (see Chapter 21 for a complete discussion of the four basic appeals)—which is the ability to reach people by putting what you want them to do in terms of what they have to gain or lose. If your opponent or customer has something to gain or lose, you have something you can use.

Simply put, the art of mediation is the ability to skillfully present options, which takes us right back to Step 3 of the Five-Step Hard Style (see Chapter 12).

THREE IN ONE

All three of what I call the great communication arts were at work in that alley that night, even though I was a beginner, feeling my way along. I wouldn't have had to represent the bartender in his complaint, but that seemed necessary to gain voluntary compliance. I chose not to insult the man or challenge him, because then I would have forced him to fight— the last thing I wanted to do.

I've clarified that empathy underlies all these arts, and I was certainly trying to empathize that night. He and I had to work together if I wanted to keep working at all. So, I had to think with him and—because he was under so many influences—I had to think for him too. Where's he coming from? What's he got to gain? What's he got to lose? What can I use? I had to think like him long enough to find the terms of my appeal.

I had to remove my ego to keep from saying something stupid like "You're not as tough as you think. I've got some black belts. I can hurt you too. Come on, try it!" That would have been counterproductive, of course, because any time a professional manifests his personal face, he forces conflict.

The art of translation was also clearly present that night. I sent my message ("Cooperate because it's best for you"), but I was using his language (time, money, job, record, and girlfriend).

The people you deal with may have other kinds of things to lose (like reputation, standing in the community or business, freedom of movement, financial options, family relationships). It's your job as professional communicator—or even an amateur Verbal Judo practitioner—to anticipate these and empathize. When you put things into context for the person, you're translating.

When I helped the mountain man see which of his options were in his best interest, I was cutting across his experience as a service to him. That was mediation, getting him to see his experience in a way that would alter his behavior.

Admittedly, my experience was from a police perspective. But isn't what I did also what we do when we deal with our children, whether trying to keep them off drugs, get them to come in early, get them to take out the trash, or get them to study? We need to sound as if we care, keep our egos out of it, find the right words to reach them, and present options that will have a powerful influence.

If you start mastering the three great arts of communication, backed by the Five-Step Hard Style, you'll be able to interact professionally with anyone anywhere under any circumstance.

16

What Makes This All So Difficult

ONE OF MY goals is to raise your expectations of yourself so you can become better tomorrow. You can learn to take more verbal abuse with greater style if you begin to see yourself as a professional who treats people with dignity and respect. You can become a Verbal Judo expert, someone who can not only represent and translate, but who can also mediate.

What makes communication so difficult is another of my undeniable, inarguable, street-survival truths: When two people are talking, six different identities are involved—each person's real self, each person as he is seen by himself, and finally, each person as seen by the other, doubled.

The way the other person sees himself is monumental for you to understand. I've never had anyone say, "I'm an idiot. I'm off the wall. I'm a jackass. I'm stupid, illiterate, and dumb, but here's what I think." People don't go around thinking they're irrational, *especially* when they truly are. So never put a person down. Focus on the goal of gaining voluntary compliance, and always allow a person to save face.

We know the least about our real selves. That's why we must deal with how we see ourselves. Our real selves may consist of where we come from, our beliefs and values, and the way we're raised. But our selves as we see them will be bogus unless we make an effort to really be honest and introspective. If we don't, we will always have areas that can be exploited and can make us less effective than we could be.

The way we are seen by others is vital, because we have a lot to say about determining that. If you consider yourself a professional, you will exude professionalism. (One of the reasons I avoid bad-mouthing and humiliating people is that I don't like myself when I do it. It's no way for a professional to act.)

When dealing with somebody in a business or a law enforcement situation, you may be thinking *I'm handling this well. I'm firm, fair, and professional.* But if the other person sees you as pushy and aggressive, as ineffective, biased, and intemperate, where does the truth lie?

Unfortunately, it lies with how you're seen and not with how you see yourself—even if you are right. I can prove it. Say I'm talking to you about a problem, and I think I'm handling you well. You do not think so, so what feedback are you going to give me? You are going to react based on how you see it, not on how I see it, and then I will have no choice. I can deal only with how you see it, even if I'm right. Otherwise, you might hit me upside the head. I'd be surprised, and you could flee, all because I was concentrating on my view of the encounter rather than yours.

What if that happens in the business world? You get a letter of complaint. Someone says you're ineffective. Someone complains to the manager and you're surprised. If you've ever been surprised by a complaint about your performance, you need some survival skill. Effective communication begins and ends with your ability to see yourself as you are seen. You desperately need the ability to read an audience and to sense from their voice and body language whether you're coming across the way you want to, so you can adjust.

So, the most important of the six selves involved in any two-person encounter is you as seen by the other. You need to develop increasingly sensitive radar to know how you're coming across while you're performing.

ELEMENTS OF COMMUNICATION

From the receiver's point of view, there are three elements of communication from which he will take his cues. The truth, which lies in the content element, carries a weight of only 7 to 10 percent of your total impact. Your very message, which you may see as the most important part of the process, is the least-considered factor.

Your voice carries a weight of 33 to 40 percent. And what I call your ONVs, other nonverbals, make up 50 to 60 percent of your impact. On the phone, where your ONVs can't come into play, content remains at 7 to 10 percent of your impact, while voice makes up the rest. Think about that. The goods, the truth, the point in these encounters is almost irrelevant compared to your voice and body language (ONVs)! The facts don't speak for themselves in court, in an arrest situation, in your office, or at home. People aren't buying what you say; they're concentrating on how you're saying it.

In spite of that, you still have to be right, because should you be wrong about a single detail, you lose credibility. Lose credibility and you lose belief. When people stop believing in you, you lose power and influence. You're history.

BABY, IT'S YOU!

If voice is so important, what do I mean by it? No guesswork here. Voice is your verbal personality as heard by the other. Remember the first time you heard your voice on a tape recorder? Like most of us, you probably said, "Hey, that doesn't sound like me! That's not me, is it?"

Bad news: That's you, baby! That's you with the monotone voice, the gravelly voice, the condescending voice, the unpleasant voice. If our voices are as powerful as research shows, we'd better know as much as we can about them, and how to improve them.

There are four elements to voice. The first, *tone,* is the most deadly four-letter word I know. Tone of voice has caused more violence, more divorce, more lost court cases, more lost business, and more brawls than anything else I can think of.

Why is tone so powerful? Because it conveys your real attitude toward people. To a customer your words may be, "Yes, sir, I'm doing everything I can to help you," but if you have a negative, condescending tone of voice to go with them, do you know what the customer hears? In his mind he tacks something onto the end of that sentence that has come through so loud and clear that he believes you said it. He hears, "I'm doing everything I can to help you, you idiot!"

If you've ever been puzzled by a complaint where somebody claimed you called him a name you had not, in fact, called him, this is why. He heard the name implied by your tone, and he heard it so clearly he'll swear you said it.

The only way to be careful enough with your voice to keep its tone from giving away your true feelings is to be sure there's harmony between the role you're playing and the voice you're using. I'm convinced that if there is any conflict between your role and your voice, people will always believe your voice. That means you must harmonize the two, and that, unfortunately, means that there are times when your voice must lie. I'm not talking about speaking an untruth. I'm talking about camouflaging a tone that would otherwise reveal your true feelings.

You're a cop and a lady asks you for directions to the convention hall. You snap, "Ma'am, you're standing right in front of it!" What does she hear in her mind at the end of that sentence? " . . . you fool!"

Now you know she didn't miss that tone. If she's a Nice Person, she just takes that insult and goes away, feeling bad. She'll say, "Thank you," and walk off, thinking, *Gee, I thought they were supposed to help me.*

If she's a Difficult Person, she'll say, "Hey, thanks a lot, Officer! Really appreciate that! Let me tell you something. I've had it with you people." Now she's in your face, and she wants your badge number. You're in deep trouble.

If she's a Wimp, you're even worse off. She takes the insult and says, "Thank you," but while she's at the convention she's sitting on that insult, and it is inflating her with righteous adrenaline. She'll be thinking, *I should have said something. This is outrageous! I don't have to put up with this.*

This woman who went in at eighty pounds is now four hundred pounds of adrenaline. She doesn't go to the party she was invited to, she goes home. She reaches for her phone or for her stationery, and you have yourself a complaint. Nice going! You did your job. You gave her the correct information, but your tone undercut your work.

A ROLE IS A ROLE IS A ROLE

Think how many roles we play in a given day. As a police officer I played enforcer, good guy, bad guy, report writer, information dispenser, tourist guide, investigator, employer, supervisor, and so on. Regardless of your occupation, at different times during the day you're probably playing mediator, translator, salesperson, customer service rep, complaint department chief, and so on.

How would you, nearly an expert at Verbal Judo by now, have handled the lady asking you for directions to the convention center—the one she was standing in front of at the time?

First, you're a chameleon, so you put on the appropriate face. She may be a dingbat, but she's not a speeder, not a criminal. She may be a nuisance, but she's a citizen, a constituent. So you smile. And you say, "Ma'am, you're in luck! Turn around and you're there. As you go through the main entrance, take an immediate right and head to Gate B. That'll get you inside the quickest, okay? You have yourself a nice evening now, and thanks for stopping by."

Now, if in reality you're a Difficult Person and a cynic, and you just have to make fun of her, wait till she turns away—hopefully with a smile and a thank-you—and you can say to your partner, "Idiot!" Just don't say it to her.

THREE OTHER ELEMENTS

Besides tone, your voice has three other elements: *pace, pitch,* and *modulation.* Pace, of course, is your speed. Pitch is how high or low and how loud and soft you speak. And modulation is your rhythm and inflection.

If you want to calm somebody, modulate your voice as you assure him, "Listen, it's going to be all right." That's a whole lot different than "Listen! I'm doing everything I can, so calm down!"

Cops also listen to pace and pitch to tell them whether people are getting more upset or coming to a decision that may not be good. If someone's voice picks up speed, watch out! He's getting excited and something may happen. If the voice slows down, he's thinking, which may be positive or negative—so be careful.

If cops can tell that much by someone else's voice characteristics, imagine what others can tell from yours. Correct and appropriate tone, pace, pitch, and modulation can help you harmonize your voice with your role, and you will be successful communicating with people.

PROXIMICS

Proximics is a fancy word for proximity, or the way you stand around and carry yourself in your space. If 50 to 60 percent of your power and effectiveness in face-to-face encounters has to do with your ONVs, it only makes sense to work on your facial expressions, how you use your hands, and how you carry yourself.

Your ONVs must harmonize with your voice. If your

voice is calming, your demeanor has to be calming. Otherwise, people will not believe what you're saying. Remember, 93 percent of your success with people has to do with your delivery and only the slightest percent has to do with *what* you say.

A mediocre idea brilliantly presented often gains acceptance, whereas a brilliant idea badly presented often dies in birth. Your success with your children, your spouse, your employees, and the public hinges on how you come across. Think of yourself as the person who can make or break your audience. Your power to persuade, to combine and harmonize your voice with your other nonverbals, can transmit the message: "I'm here to serve you," because you convince your hearer that you care about what you're saying.

LIGHTS, CAMERA, ACTING!

The presentation of self is terribly important. If I had my way, I'd send everyone to acting school before having him or her deal with the public and perform eight to ten hours a day. But that's not feasible, so stay with me, pick up on the principles and tactics of Verbal Judo, and you will find yourself more effective almost overnight.

17

Readin', 'Ritin', and Rhetoric

To BE A good persuader, you have to learn to read your opponent and the situation. Much like my old Indian mentor taught me to read a trail when I was six or seven years old, I would like to teach you to read people and size up a verbal encounter.

Because my doctorate is in English literature, a classical discipline, I feel the need to put things in rhetorical perspective. But don't feel intimidated. I'm also an earthy guy. Highfalutin as it may sound, rhetorical perspective is easily defined and helps put handles on the subject of this chapter.

Rhetoric is an interesting word often used in the modern idiom to mean a bunch of words and no substance, such as "That's just rhetoric." But the word has classical roots. Used by Aristotle, it was a word of dignity. It meant "the art of verbal appeal or verbal persuasion."

To me, rhetoric is the art of finding the right means and the right words to generate voluntary compliance. Rhetoric *is* Verbal Judo.

THE THIRD "R"

Rhetoric was actually a subject taught in the American public school system up until about 1940 or so, and I, for one, wouldn't mind seeing it return to the classroom. Even if the concept is foreign to you, open your mind to it. I want to give you a rhetorical perspective on communication, persuasion, and generating voluntary compliance.

I have developed an acronym—PAVPO—which I agree is kind of an ugly-sounding one, but which is also very serviceable. If you can lock it into your mind, it will help you memorize the five components of what I call the rhetorical perspective of Verbal Judo, some of which I have already discussed:

Perspective
Audience
Voice
Purpose
Organization

If you can develop and use a rhetorical perspective in your daily life, you'll be far more skillful and effective as a communicator.

Perspective

Perspective is simply the way you see things, your point of view, based on your knowledge, your understanding of the situation, your background, and your experience. You have to know what you're talking about to either a group or an individual. That means you have mastered your policies, your procedures, your products, what you can and cannot do.

Too many people believe that preparing what they want

to say is the end-all of effective communication. As important as that is, disregarding the other areas is an error, as I will show you. But first let me address this issue of your own point of view.

The more thoroughly you know what you know, the more powerfully you will present it. You will have an aura of certainty that comes only with preparation. There is no substitute for knowing what you want to say and having the data to back it up.

For example, if I go before the city council to appeal for more money for my budget area, I will spend what time is necessary gathering my data and creating charts that compare my department with others. My evidence and arguments will be all marshaled. I will be prepared to control my emotions and biases and to plead my case from a position of strength.

My perspective, based on my expertise, will come through because I know what I'm talking about and I'm under control.

Audience

Many people, after their preparation, just go out before an audience and begin to speak, but that's a crucial blunder. You must spend equal time considering your audience, analyzing to whom you will be speaking.

Who are these people on the city council, for example? If there are eight people on the council, I must study all eight individually. What are their values, their belief systems? How do they think? Who are their constituents? What will their objections likely be?

I have to think carefully from their point of view. Once again, that powerful word *empathy* comes into play. I want to think like the others, put myself into their shoes, anticipate their reactions based on my knowledge of the positions from which they will be listening.

Depending on my reading of these people I may open differently. For example, if I know that they're highly analytical people or that at least several are antagonistic, I will probably open with a series of examples of data comparison, factually showing that my need for money is real.

If I have determined there is no one that highly analytical in the audience, I might try another approach altogether. If it's kind of a good ol' boy city council, I might start out being much more chatty and informal. If they are self-righteous and see me as an underling who should be deferential, I'll be that and maybe a little self-effacing with some self-deprecating humor. When they're impressed and know that I know my place, I will earnestly prove my need for funds and hope for the best.

Whether you're speaking to a roomful of citizens, a city council of eight, or just one disgruntled customer, you are onstage. You are playing a role before others, and you should be aware of the dynamics of each situation. For example, when I teach I often suddenly pull a camera out of my bag and point it at the students.

Immediately the room changes. Everything becomes still and silent, and then there's some nervous giggling, people looking down, others warily looking at that camera, wondering what I'm doing with it. Think of yourself as that camera. As you enter a scene, it changes.

You can make two assumptions right off the bat. First, people will always see differently than you. I don't care whether you've been married two or twenty years, your spouse does not think the way you do. The moment you begin to believe that he or she does, you're headed for problems. Never assume people are going to agree with you 100 percent.

Second, as you enter, you're very much like an actor appearing onstage. The audience quiets and they watch.

When I walked into a bar as a police officer, the whole place hushed. People whispered, "Cops!" or "The police are here." People's behavior changed. They tried to surreptitiously hide contraband, and say, "Oh yes. Evening, Officer. Oh yes. Evening." Even if they were clearly up to no good, they were doing their best to appear otherwise.

Not only did they change as I entered the bar, but they also watched me. Again, it was as if I had walked onstage. They watched as I performed.

You must think of yourself as a performer, whether before your children, your spouse, or your constituency (citizens, customers, whomever). If you can see yourself as someone who is there to make changes as you act, you will understand a most interesting point, first made by Aristotle, that audiences are made, not found.

If an actor does a poor job and the audience says he's terrible, it makes no difference that the actor thinks he did a brilliant job. How he sees himself, remember, is not as important as how he's seen. If an audience thinks you're boring, you are. If an audience thinks you don't know what you're talking about, you don't. You've got a problem. You've failed to perform in such a way as to get their attention. More than likely you failed to analyze in advance who those people really are, what they might think, what they might anticipate, what their objections might be. If you had, then as you entered the scene your walk and your voice would have appropriately matched their needs.

Voice

See Chapter 16.

Purpose

Purpose is, of course, your bottom line: the result you must professionally achieve. If you do everything else right and don't achieve your purpose, obviously, you've failed. You'd be surprised at the number of people who go into a presentation or an argument concerned only with preparing, or knowing their audience, or using their voice properly, and being satisfied that they have done all these things—only to realize later that they did not achieve their purpose. If all you care about is the means and not the end, you'll be thrilled if you perform well. As for me, I'm into results. I want to see the purpose achieved, even if everything else doesn't go perfectly.

If, however, you have a handle on perspective, audience, and voice, your purpose will likely be fulfilled. One way to ensure that you'll be effective is to concentrate on the last letter in my homely, but hopefully effective acronym.

Organization

Organization is simply how you want the encounter to unfold from beginning to middle to end. The responsibility for ordering the event is yours, and you will, of course, organize it based on your reading of the situation.

Nowhere did I learn more clearly the importance of this component than on the streets as a cop. Let me use yet another police example, because I believe it is easy to transfer the principles to your situation. Police work represents the essence of Verbal Judo in stark clarity. In other words, if it doesn't work on the street, you can't use it at home or at the office.

Take the average, everyday, nonfelony car stop. At one time or another you have likely been stopped by the police, so you can identify with this and compare it with your experience.

The average police officer not trained in tactical communication tends to approach a car and immediately snap, "Let me see your driver's license!"

To which the driver often responds, "Why? What have I done? Why are you stopping me?"

Notice that all the initial verbal conflict arises from the fact that the officer asked for the driver's license first. What if he asked for it later, anticipated the questions, and answered them before they were asked? (One of my pet peeves is the officer who studies the license and then asks, "Do you know why I stopped you?" What is that? A quiz? Most fully functioning adults know a setup when they see one. Who's going to give him what he needs to write a ticket? The obvious answer, even if you have an idea what you might have done, is "No, why did you stop me?" What does the cop expect? Surely not an answer like "Yes, Officer, I know why you stopped me. I was speeding, driving recklessly, ignoring stop signs, and drinking in the car.)

However, I teach across the country what I call a Nine-Step Car Stop. It has a far different order from the way most officers are trained. It goes like this:

1. **Greeting.** "Good evening, sir/ma'am." I say it with sincerity and a smile. More than likely I'm dealing with a normal citizen, not a dangerous criminal. Pleasantly I break the ice.

2. **Identification of yourself and department.** "I'm Officer Thompson of the Home Town Police Department." That should make me sound as if I know what I'm doing. I'm establishing command presence, clarity, and an unafraid approach. I've offered my title (officer), my name, and my authority (the name of my department).

   We know from research that when you give your name, you personalize the encounter to the point where you can expect less verbal abuse. Once I have given my name, it becomes harder for the citizen to start calling me names and treating me like some abstract, uniformed, unknown authority person. Names have a way of calming people. Too often we use numbers and titles rather than names. In a store, doesn't it help if the clerk at the counter introduces himself and says, "Hi, I'm Bill. How can I help you?"

3. **Reason for the stop.** "The reason I stopped you is that I did pace you over the last four blocks at forty-five miles per hour in a twenty zone." Notice I've given the reason right up front, even before asking for the license. Then I move immediately into the next step.

4. **Justification.** "Is there some reason for such excessive speed this evening?" Normally the answer is dead silence, because it's hard to say anything without convicting yourself. But if you're bleeding and taking yourself to the hospital or your wife is having a baby

in the car, there just might be justification for exceeding the speed limit. In such a case, the officer will escort you to your destination as quickly as is safe. When, however, there is no answer to the justification question, I can go right on to the next step.

5. **Request license, papers, and cooperation.** "May I see your driver's license?"

By now the encounter, rather than starting as usual with this threatening step, sounds more like "Good evening, sir/ma'am. I'm Officer Thompson of the Home Town Police Department. The reason I stopped you is that I did pace you over the last four blocks at forty-five miles per hour in a twenty zone. Is there some reason for such excessive speed this evening? If not, I will need to see your driver's license."

Not only does that sound polite, but notice that also there is a command presence. I sound knowledgeable, I sound clear, I sound professional. Also there's no personal challenge or a snapping at the citizen.

Perhaps most important, look what the driver can no longer say.

"Why are you stopping me?" I've told him.

"Who do you think you are?" I've even told him that, and it's not who *I* think I am; I'm acting under the authority of the city.

By anticipating certain kinds of abuse and questions, I have ordered my presentation to deflect them. I have taken those weapons away from my opponent and made him less of an opponent and more of an ally. I basically have sounded professional without having angered the citizen.

As kind and professional as that approach is, it is also very forceful, and these five steps will usually persuade the person to produce a driver's license.

6. **Clarification.** If there's anything more I need to know

(Is this your current address? Is there anything I can help you with?), I ask it now.

7. **Decision.** There are only three things a police officer can do. He can warn you and let you go, cite you with a ticket, or move to the optional next step.

8. **Search and seize.** This step is necessary only if the officer sees contraband or discovers that your car is stolen, you're wanted for some other offense, or you create a disturbance by physically resisting. That, of course, is rare.

9. **Close.** My goal here is to effectively and appropriately close the encounter so you feel better about it than you did at first. If I issue you a ticket, I will say, "Thank you for your cooperation. Do drive carefully." If I have given you a warning, I will say, "Have a nice day." Notice that I don't say, "Have a nice day," if I've given you a ticket, because I just cost you money and would thus sound sarcastic.

Look at the advantages of the Nine-Step Car Stop and apply them to your typical confrontations.

It's polite.

It normally generates voluntary compliance.

Its structure creates presence for you and deflects verbal abuse.

If this approach fails and abuse is still coming your way, you can immediately switch to Step 2 (setting context) of the Five-Step Hard Style outlined in Chapter 12. If that doesn't work, move to confirmation ("Is there anything I can say or do to get you to cooperate?"). If the answer is no, you must take action. I hope it never gets to that point for you, unless you are in law enforcement and have all the resources you need to coerce compliance.

This structured, professional approach should keep you safe and sounding good, even when you may be having a bad day. The professional communicator can't let bad days get to him. Under pressure, the pro just gets better.

That ninth step, the appropriate close, should be memorized to the point where it's second nature and can be enacted even when you don't like the person you're dealing with. The ninth step keeps you safe because you sound professional. It allows you to ignore your negative inner voice, which would have you give that speech you would live to regret.

BUT I'M A CIVILIAN

Fair enough. You don't have at your disposal the uniform, the law, the tactics, the weapons of a cop. Your problem is not a speeder or a dangerous lawbreaker. Maybe you're in a business, dealing with a complaining customer who is clearly overreacting and out of control.

First, make it your goal, your business, to win the person over. No matter what is said, you're going to deflect the abuse, not take it personally, remain professional, and keep your eyes on the purpose. You want what the customer wants: satisfaction and a happy result. Let nothing stand in the way of that.

Can you see the transferable principles from PAVPO and even several from the Nine-Step Car Stop? You have perspective because you have mastered your policies, your procedures, your products, what you can and cannot do. You have that aura of certainty that comes only with preparation. Remember that there is no substitute for knowing what you want to say and having the data to back it up.

You have an audience you may not have had time to study, but take whatever time you can to research them anyway. If you're on the phone with a disgruntled customer, try to bring the account up on your computer or stall for enough time to pull it from the file. Anything you can learn about the person or the account will help in how you deal with him. "I hope we can straighten this out for you so that you can enjoy the product as much as you have the garden tractor. Is that still working out for you?"

Or if you see a previous return in the file, you might ask if the reimbursement arrived in due time and apologize for any delay.

Clearly your voice in such an encounter should be soothing and authoritative. You're as apologetic as necessary, as confident as you can be, and reassuring—insisting that the customer finally has the right person and that by the time you are finished, action will have been taken.

Your purpose was determined as soon as you silently set your mind to satisfying this customer. Obviously there is a limit to what you can do, and that limit is the integrity and well-being of your business. But when you know what kind of damage one unhappy customer can do to a company, that expands the horizon of possibilities. Your purpose is to turn a bad situation into a good one, an unhappy customer into a happy one. Many management experts will tell you that it is better to have a satisfactorily repaired relationship with a customer than a relationship that has never had a hitch. Such results are talked about among friends, and people take notice.

Organization, you'll recall, is how you want the situation to unfold. That is in your hands. Don't let the customer dictate it. When a customer starts raising his voice or making accusations, that is the time to take charge. With your best voice, tell him, "I am absolutely certain we can work this out to your complete satisfaction." Then go immediately into your variation of my car stop steps. "My name is _____ , and my job here is to get to the bottom of just these types of matters. Let me tell you what information will be most helpful in being sure this is taken care of."

Once everything has been clarified, you can present options. "Based on what you've told me, here is what I am prepared to do. By policy, I can refund your money, replace the item, or give you the appropriate credit in your account. Which would be best for you?"

The appropriate close will tell you whether the person has been completely satisfied. "Will that take care of it? Is there anything else we can do for you?"

WORTH MEMORIZING

Jot my rhetorical approach on a card and carry it with you until you have memorized it: PAVPO—*P*erspective, *A*udience, *V*oice, *P*urpose, and *O*rganization.

18

How to Diagnose a Verbal Encounter

You'll find I'm big on acronyms, anything that will help me remember what to do and when and how to do it. Another one that can help you diagnose a verbal encounter and thus skillfully deal with people under pressure is PACE: *P*roblem (situation you're in), *A*udience (to whom are you speaking), *C*onstraints (obstacles to effective communication), and *E*thical presence (your professional face).

PROBLEM

How do you size up what's facing you?

I answered a call one night that a man was holding his son hostage with a knife. His apartment was surrounded by the SWAT team, and the man was in a corner about twenty feet from the door, holding a knife to the throat of his son, who appeared about six or seven years old.

As I approached the door, which was partially barricaded, the man shouted, "Stay where you are, pig! I'll kill you and the boy!"

147

I stopped and held up my hands. "Whoa!" I said, "I'm not coming any closer. What's the matter, sir?"

He said, "I have to kill my boy."

I said, "What do you mean you have to kill your boy? You don't have to kill him. There are many things you can do besides kill him, aren't there?"

"No, I've gotta kill my boy."

"Well, tell me about it."

He said, "My boy's possessed of the devil. My ex-wife was a she-devil and she poisoned his soul, poisoned his blood, and I've gotta blood-let him. I've gotta cleanse him, cut his throat and cleanse him or the devil will take him forever."

Here I am, a professional at the door, thinking, *This guy's crazy.*

Clearly, I had a problem, and it wasn't hard to define. The crazy man was the problem, and my job was to take the knife away, save the boy's life, and arrest the man. The thing is, there are always two kinds of problems in any difficult encounter: your problem, as you define it as a professional, and the problem from the other person's point of view.

If I had stopped at my problem and begun my discourse there, I'd have yet a third problem, bigger than either of the two I had already. I saw the man as the problem; he saw the boy as the problem. If I had approached him as if he were the problem, he would have merely disagreed and resisted, and at worse killed the boy and maybe some of us cops in the process.

This is the epitome of what I call the rhetorical problem: how the other person sees it. And he will never see it the way you do, especially if he's crazy (or under any other influence or delusion). I've learned the hard way that the only way to succeed in these situations is to define the problem from the other person's point of view *first.*

Frankly, the first thing I said to the man was wholly ineffective. I said, "But, sir, wait a minute. The blood that runs in the boy's veins runs in yours. If you cut his throat, that's your identity going into the floorboards as well as his. Think about it."

He wasn't buying. He screamed, "No! I said the blood was poisoned. It's poisoned!"

So I came at him a different way, with a new kind of appeal. "But wait a minute! Why would you give your ex-wife power? She'd love to see you kill the thing you love the most in order to save it. That only makes her look good and feel good. But it takes from you the very thing you love."

I thought that was a pretty powerful argument because I was looking at it from only my point of view. I certainly wouldn't kill someone I loved in order to save him.

But my approach angered the man. He zoomed from a seven to a nine on the emotional scale of one to ten. *Good work, Thompson.* He jiggled the knife at his son's throat and said, "She's a dead woman anyway. I'm going to kill her later."

Finally I came to my senses and began to try to work with instead of against the man. I said, "Whoa! Wait a minute! What if I told you, sir, that I know a priest, who by just passing his hands over your boy can get the evil spirits out? That way, you keep the thing you love the most, and your ex-wife loses."

He looked at me for a minute, clearly stunned. "Do you really know somebody like that?"

And I said, "You bet I do! He owes me some favors. Listen, let me talk to him and see if we can get him here."

"But I can't trust you, you're a cop!"

I candidly didn't know what to do with that at the moment, so I deflected it with a strip phrase. "Sir, I 'preciate that, but trust is not an issue at this point. [Imagine the absurdity of that! But it worked.] I can't help you. I stand before you unarmed for good reason. Only the priest can help you." To make a long story short, he put the knife down.

If I had dwelt on my perspective (that the man was the problem), even though I was right, I couldn't have helped. I had to see the problem as he did so I could seem to be working with him to get it solved. That also saved the boy's life, so mission accomplished. While it may have seemed absurd for me to buy into his craziness of seeing the boy as the problem, I did it for the greater benefit.

AUDIENCE

The question in this context is how your audience differs
from you. What made that man different from me? How did
he see the event differently? What were his values and beliefs?
Of course, he was crazy, but that didn't help me analyze the
situation. The big difference between us was his belief system.
He was highly superstitious. I have my superstitions, and with
my history of an Indian influencing my childhood, attending
a Quaker high school, and assimilating Eastern influences
through the martial arts, I have my own views of spirituality.
But superstitious I'm not. I had to keep that in mind when
I negotiated with the man.

CONSTRAINTS

Just about anything can be considered a constraint, but in
this case, clearly this man's rage, his brain damage, his influence, his belief systems, all were obstacles. There is only one
of three things you can do with a restraint: step around it,
ignore it, or use it. I ignored his hatred and distrust of cops.
I let his threat to kill me fly by (Remember, "Man throws
spear at head, move head . . . ").

I stepped around his mistrust with a strip phrase and
got to the heart of the matter. Had he been thinking ration-
ally, he would have known that trust was the whole point
here. Was I going to help him or thwart him? You know
what my goal was.

No, the major constraint was his superstition, and when
I finally tapped into that, I had found the answer. I appealed
to and used the very thing that had made him difficult to
talk to in the first place. In other words, if he believed blood-
letting would take care of poisoned blood, he'd certainly go
for a religious ceremony that would do the same without
hurting his son.

Knowing what makes your audience different from you allows you to adapt, show empathy, and work with them. If they're in left field, you've got to use left-field language.

ETHICAL PRESENCE

Notice that throughout my dealings with the man, I tried to exude ethical presence, a concern. I was saying, in effect, "I'm working with you, sir. Listen to me." If I couldn't convince him of that, I was going to fail for sure.

That is why it is so important to keep your professional face in front. Show concern at all times. Again, sometimes you're bluffing, and frankly, I don't apologize for misleading an easily misled crazy person who is a threat to someone else's life. If you consider yourself a scrupulously honest person and think I'm advocating situational ethics here, you're right. But ask yourself: If a crazed man with a butcher knife broke into your house and asked you where your baby was, would you feel obligated to tell the truth? I hope not.

The fact was, I didn't know a priest. We did get the man the psychiatric help he needed, but I had said whatever I needed to to get that boy out of that traumatic situation.

In spite of that, remember that in its everyday application Verbal Judo is not about conning people. Con men use words to raise your expectations, and then they use those expectations to cheat you for their own profit.

The goal of Verbal Judo, on the other hand, is to benefit both parties in a confrontation. Use PACE with your spouse and with your children. Use it in the workplace. The next time you have an argument, before you start snapping back and using your words to address your own feelings, why not stop and analyze. What is the problem? How does my opponent see it? How is my opponent different from me? What constraints make it so difficult to deal with him today? And remember to keep a concerned and caring face. That in itself is often enough to deflect abuse.

19

The Language of Reassurance

FANCY AND COMPLICATED research goes into the subject of communication all the time, and many experts consider it a complex topic. As the founder of Verbal Judo, I am amazed at the simplicity of communication. Even I have had to codify and systematize the discipline, but I've found that if you learn the underlying principles, you don't need to remember every detail of the training.

Consider the language of calming people down, what I call the language of reassurance. There may be a hundred different ways to calm people, but I believe there's only one principle that underlies all those techniques. It consists of three words—Empathy Absorbs Tension—and one of them, as you will see, is one of my favorite hobbyhorses.

If you can project understanding, empathy, you will absorb like a sponge the tension of your child, your spouse, or anyone else you're dealing with.

When I say there are hundreds of techniques to do this, I'm referring to all those little things people do that prove that it works. In other words, no matter what approach you choose, if the result somehow shows empathy, tension will

153

be absorbed, and you have begun to succeed in Verbal Judo. Can't remember one of my acronyms? Do something to empathize. Forgot which step comes next in a list of suggestions? Empathize, empathize, empathize. Regardless what you do, if you don't absorb tension, you will fail. Use this book as a manual, a reminder, a source. But get the principles clearly in your mind so that when you're in the heat of battle you're doing the right thing even if you're not going about it the precise way I or one of my instructors would.

You'd think I would have my whole course memorized, as many times as I've taught it. And if I were forced at gunpoint to regurgitate it, I probably could. But even I fall back on the basic principles sometimes, when there's simply no opportunity to carefully weigh options and remember steps.

THE CAP AND THE CARD

I was on the street for a ride-along in California one night when Ron, the police officer I was with, arrested a subject on a minor felony warrant. The perpetrator was about sixteen years old. At about 3:00 A.M., the boy's mother was standing on her porch, shouting obscenities. The officer, one of the most skillful I've ever seen, put the kid in the car, turned to me in the front seat, and said, "I'll be with you in a moment, George."

Frankly I wished he'd jumped into the patrol car and we were gone because the woman's yelling had attracted more than a dozen angry neighbors. Their sleep had been interrupted by these cops, who had, in their minds, hassled some innocent kid they'd seen grow up on that street. They came out sniffing the air like Doberman pinschers. It was as if they were asking themselves, "Is there something here for me? Anything I need to stick my nose into? What's going on here?"

I was tense because those people were surrounding the car. They weren't saying anything, but it was an uneasy, potentially explosive situation. Suddenly, Ron walked up to the woman, took off his hat, put it under his arm as if he had all night, reached into his pocket for a business card, and said, "Ma'am, listen to me. My name is Officer Ron _____, and I'm with the _____ Police Department. I'm arresting your boy because I have to. I have a warrant. If I don't arrest him, they arrest me. But it's a minor warrant, ma'am.

"I don't blame you for being upset, because I have a son about your boy's age, and I'd be upset too. But he'll be out in the morning. Listen, don't stand out here tonight. Get some rest. Come on down to the police department in the morning, bring your friends, bring a lawyer if you want. Your son will have been processed by then and you'll be able to talk to him.

"And look, if anyone gives you any trouble down there, you call my number, and I'll take care of it. You don't deserve any more problems. You have a good night now."

He turned and walked away, putting his hat back on, and we drove off while the woman was thanking him! Her son was cuffed in the back of that car, and she was grateful!

I was astounded! That woman was on the porch, hands on her hips, mouth open, virtually speechless. No more virulence, no more obscenities, she was just staring as we pulled away. The people who had surrounded the car were quiet, everybody watching. I could have applauded. Imagine how much safer Ron would be if he had to go back into that neighborhood the next night to make an arrest.

Everything Ron did showed respect and dignity. Later I asked him about the hat and the card business. He said, "The hat's an old trick, George. I sometimes forget to show proper verbal respect because I'm busy or we're rushed. So I wear the hat. You take the hat off, it shows people respect. The more difficult the neighborhood, the more important respect is."

I nodded. "What about that card?"

He said, "That card's interesting, isn't it? Number one, when I hand her the card, that shows I'm a professional. Shows I'm not afraid about what I'm doing. Second, even though I invited her to call me with any complaints, you know she probably won't. But still I *might* hear from her. I've made more good felony arrests over the years with those cards, 'cause I've left them all over the community.

"That woman is apt to call me a year from now and say, 'Officer Ron, you remember me? You arrested my boy last October on that minor felony warrant? Why aren't you out here cracking down on these people selling drugs right out the back door of number one-twelve every day between four and five in the morning?'

"Well, I thank her, and I get on it, and usually these people are right. Their leads are good. The cards have helped me cultivate a beat."

I noticed he said "*cultivate* a beat" not "*run* a beat," and I thought how lucky that city was to have a guy like Ron on the streets.

You may not wear a hat or even carry business cards. That's why the principle is more important than the specific technique. How many ways are there to show empathy and concern and to absorb tension?

"CALM DOWN AND SPEAK ENGLISH!"

Now a surefire way to escalate tension is to break a cardinal rule of calming someone (by shouting, "Calm down!") and insult him in the process. I inherited a problem that began that way one night.

I drove into the police station to begin my shift when I came upon an older officer trying to deal with a young Japanese girl who was hysterical. She was crying and shouting at him in unintelligible half Pidgin English and half Japanese. He was upset and shouting right back at her, "Calm down and speak English! How can I help you if I can't understand you? What's the matter with you?"

As soon as he saw me he saw his chance to finish his shift and get home. "You there!" he said. "You come and deal with her. I haven't got any idea what she's sayin', and I'm outta here!"

Then he was gone and she was in my face. Almost instinctively, because there certainly was no book on this subject back then, I reached into my pocket and came out with my black book and pen and handed them to her. "Here, ma'am," I said quietly. "Write. Write down problem."

As she grabbed the book and the pen I noticed three things. Number one, she had stopped yelling. You can't yell and write at the same time.

Number two, what she had in her hands was tangible evidence that someone had time for her, cared about her, wanted to help her, and would work on her problem—whatever it was.

Number three, I realized that it didn't make much difference what she wrote. If she couldn't make herself understood when she spoke, I doubted I would be able to read a thing she put on that page. My guess and my hope was that if I could get her busy helping me get the message, it would calm her enough that I could make some sense of it.

When she handed the book back to me, I played my Lieutenant Columbo role. I squinted at it, held it up to the light, looked at her, nodded, looked back at it, and basically counted to ten. My looking interested in what she had written seemed to calm her. When I finally tucked the book away, I said in as fatherly a tone as possible, "What'sa matter?"

By now she had calmed down enough to get three words out I could understand. "Boyfriend in there!" she said, pointing at our jail.

I motioned to her and said, "Come, come. Come with me." I took her inside, found out that her boyfriend had just been released, and was able to tell her, "Not here. Not here. Go home."

She was so grateful, thanking me over and over.

I didn't know it at the time, but that was real service. I had used a technique, making use of tactile objects to indicate concern. My empathy had absorbed the tension.

How many different techniques are there like the book and the pen or the hat and the card? People to whom English is a second or third language will resort to their own tongue when they get upset. Their communication skills abandon them, and it's up to you and me to find creative ways to calm them. I never knew such things when I was teaching English, because I didn't have to. On the street I had to come up with a hundred such techniques.

PRINCIPALLY, STICK TO THE PRINCIPLES

When I studied physical judo and jujitsu I discovered that the fighting arts, which are complicated in terms of their numerous techniques, are also very simple in terms of bottom-line principles.

For example, one of the major principles in empty-hand control is "Go to a weak area when grabbed." In other words, if someone grabs your wrist, turn it back toward his thumb, the weakest area. You can slip away easily.

That's much like the principle I'm talking about. There may be a hundred ways to calm people, but the bottom line is, empathy absorbs tension. If you keep that in your mind when you deal with your children, your spouse, or an angry customer, you'll be able to use my other techniques with ease and skill. You don't need to remember my specific suggestions, because whatever you do to show empathy and absorb tension will be right.

For instance, a woman friend of mine, picnicking with her family in a forest preserve, came upon a scene where a toddler had wandered off. He was not yet two years old, his parents each thought the other was watching him, and he'd disappeared. The rangers had been notified and they immediately went to the pool and to a stream to be sure he would not drown. Other volunteers began combing the woods.

But the young mother, panicky, turned her anger on her husband, who was shaken. "How could you let him out of your sight?" she demanded. "He's a baby!"

"You think I did it on purpose? I thought he was with you!"

The temptation might have been to shush these two, to tell them, "Knock it off! You're not helping find your child by bitching at each other!"

But my friend was wise. She separated them and calmed the mother. A total stranger, she approached the wife and embraced her. She didn't know specific steps, but she instinctively knew the principle that empathy absorbs tension. She said, "Whenever one of my babies wandered off I froze [immediate empathy and a calming influence, i.e., this is a common occurrence]. The only thing I could do was to turn my full attention to finding her, and I didn't give up until I did. And let me tell you something, I always found her [reassurance]."

The mother immediately came to her senses and joined a search party. The child was found shortly, having strayed to another picnic where a clown was entertaining. No one noticed him there until the searchers came looking.

My point is that following the exact steps and stages is less consequential than knowing the principles.

20

How to Fight Fair

A LIFE OF PEACE and harmony is a worthy goal, and there are still some people who think it's possible to live that way 100 percent of the time. This probably won't be big news to you, but to them I say, "Welcome to the real world."

A good, clean fight can change a negative situation to a positive one and release tension. Sometimes, you just have to get into it with somebody to clear the air, don't you? One or the other of you is itching for a fight—I'm speaking, of course, of a verbal, not physical, tussle here—and the only solution is to have at it.

Keeping feelings bottled up results in frustrations being expressed in weird and inappropriate ways. Have you ever wondered why you or your spouse seem bitchy and mean-spirited about things that seem to have nothing to do with anything? That's a description of someone who needs to deal with the issues at hand. A clean, effective verbal confrontation is designed to strengthen, rather than damage, a relationship. I want to teach you to express hostile feelings without humiliating or destroying others in the process.

FOUR STEPS TO A GOOD DOMESTIC DISPUTE

What's the goal of a fight at home? Most people think it's to win, but if you think that, you're brain-damaged. (How's that for a nice, Verbal Judo samurai way of breaking it to you?) But seriously, the goal is not to win, because my experience is that you cannot win a domestic dispute. Oh, you may win temporarily, but you'll find yourself sleeping in the pickup truck or apologizing the next day.

No, think about it. Fighting is not bad, if you keep in mind that the goal is to strengthen the relationship, to draw yourselves closer by having the freedom to argue without destroying each other.

The prototype I recommend to help you generate closure and keep the higher goal in mind (long-term harmony) does not lend itself to an acronym. It simply goes like this: (1) Paraphrase. (2) Paraphrase again. (3) Refocus the other's attention. (4) Say what you want to say.

Let's say a man marries for a second time and he inherits four children from his wife's first marriage. They've now been married about two months, so he still feels in a bit of a honeymoon glow, thinking things are moving along swimmingly, despite tripping over the offspring now and then.

One day he arrives home after a difficult day at work, and his wife hits him with "You know, I'm getting sick of you. Every time you come home and sit down to dinner, you do everything you can to purposely undermine me with my children. Remember, they are my children and not yours, and I'm fed up with your trying to make me look bad in front of them!"

Now notice that she broke a cardinal rule of Verbal Judo, using absolute phrases like "Every time . . ." and "purposely," so his first inclination might be to strike back with Verbal Karate. If he does, they've got a real donnybrook on their hands. He could say, "I do not! I didn't do that last night." Or, "How can you say I've done that on purpose? I didn't even know I had ever done that!" Or, "Why didn't you tell me? Am I supposed to read your mind?"

The guy is probably reeling for the reason most of us would reel in the same situation. We aren't aware we've offended or have even been an irritation to anyone. We go merrily about our business, thinking everyone is thrilled to be in our presence, only to be blindsided by what we think are spurious, mean-spirited charges.

Here's what I would recommend to the husband who's just been brought back to reality by his new, and frustrated, wife.

1. Paraphrase

First employing a trusty Sword of Insertion like "Whoa!" follow with "Wait a minute, darling [totally without sarcasm— you're reaffirming your affection, even in the heat of battle, subliminally establishing that your goal is to make things right and maintain the relationship]. Let me be sure I hear what you're saying. [Here comes the paraphrase.] You're angry at me because you think I come home every night and do everything I can to purposely undermine you in front of the children. Is that the way you feel?"

Notice how disinterested is the tone; there's no condemnation or put-down at the end of that, implied or otherwise. If I'm right, what the husband will hear next will be some sort of a modification, a softening of the original charge, because people rarely mean exactly what they say when they're angry. One of the only reasons this would not be forthcoming would be if the husband had implied in his paraphrase any sarcasm or undue emphasis on words like "you think." If those are hit too hard, the wife may react in anger, "I don't *think;* I *know!*" On the other hand, the husband has to phrase it that way so he's not admitting that whatever he did he did on purpose.

If all goes well, the wife will likely say something like "Well, I don't know if you do it every night, but you have sure done it the last three nights." Now it's time for the next step.

2. Paraphrase Again

"Okay, darling, you're angry at me because for the last three nights I have come home and purposely tried to undermine you in front of your children."

Now he's apt to hear yet another slight modification. "Well, I don't know if you purposely meant to do it, but you sure got the job done!"

With just a little careful, loving counteraction, the husband has already seen his disgruntled wife lower her charge from "you always purposely do this" to "at least you did it the last three nights and I'm not saying it was on purpose."

That's a significant modification. She has been cooled a hundred degrees. So now it's time for the next step.

3. Refocus the other's attention

Still in a conciliatory tone, the husband should now say something like "Let me ask you something. What specifically did I do the last three nights that led you to believe I was trying to undermine you?"

After a pause while she thinks about it, he will likely be hit with some serious data. "Well, you did A, B, and C! That's what you did!" Now he has something concrete to work with.

4. Say What You Want to Say

Now is the most crucial time in the argument. The husband needs to state his case, all the while convincing his wife that he has the relationship at heart. In himself he might want only to defend himself, to react in anger for being what he feels is falsely accused. But he's a Verbal Judo expert. He knows that if she perceives something, it's true in her mind and he has to deal with it, even if she's wrong.

This is another of those times to bury the ego, take a

lump or two, and concentrate on persuading your opponent that you're as interested in preserving the relationship as she is.

So, he says, "Let me ask you something, hon. Could we talk about the difference between what I do and what I intend to do? I didn't marry you two months ago to destroy the relationship, but I'm doing something wrong. Can we talk about it?"

Now unless the wife is impossible, he's going to get some cooperation. She wanted to be heard, and clearly he has heard her. Isn't that what most people want when they yell and scream? His voice should sound as though he cares. He should be using everything he knows about pace and pitch and modulation and tone.

The bottom-line message that will turn this fight into making up comes when he tells her, in one form or another: "I love you. I don't want to make you mad. I certainly don't want to undermine you in front of your children or even appear that I am. I'm sorry. Forgive me, and tell me how I can change so you'll know I'm serious about this."

Whenever there is a domestic conflict, one of the parties is going to be more difficult than the other, more under the influence than the other, more unreasonable just then. Spouses will often change roles depending on their distractions and how their day has gone. One day, he's the angry bear and she's trying to be rational and keep the peace. The next day, it's the other way around.

To me one of the great signs of true love is the ability to take over and cover for the other when he or she is having a bad day. The hope is that he or she will do the same for you when you need it.

I've been through enough broken relationships to know I learned this stuff the hard way. Simple and logical as it is, no one ever said, "George, stay calm, do not express your ego. Paraphrase. Try to get at what your wife feels and means. See if you've got it right before you react."

It was only when I began to transfer Verbal Judo tactics and skills from the street to the home that I realized these principles cross all lines and barriers. You don't have to be a cop facing down a junkie in an alley to use Verbal Judo to your benefit. You can use it at home.

If you have burned bridges, alienated people, and lost marriages, families, and credibility, maybe now is the time to start using these techniques to preserve some relationships.

Does my four-step model always work? Will it guarantee a lifetime marriage? I can't say that. But I believe it will work most of the time. The key lies with the depth of your sincerity, which is hard to combat. If you are committed to the relationship to the point where you are willing to bury your ego and get at what's really bothering your spouse, trust me, this will work.

21

Take the Giant LEAPS

I HAVE IDENTIFIED five basic tools to generate voluntary compliance, and—you guessed it—they fit into an acronym: LEAPS.

Listen
Empathize
Ask
Paraphrase
Summarize

Some of these I have already dealt with in detail, and of course all of them have been mentioned in one or another related context. But in this chapter I want to review the importance of each of these tools. Each is distinct. Anytime you communicate with anyone, you're using one or more of these, not necessarily in any particular order. So, though I have fit them into the acronym for easier remembering, I don't want you to think of them as sequential. Rather, think of them as ongoing, changing skills you must use to be effective with people, especially those under pressure. Let's take them one at a time.

LISTEN

When you listen you've got to look like you're listening. Project a face that makes it obvious. Frankly, if I had to choose between listening carefully and appearing to listen carefully, I'd opt for the latter. People often say things that are not worth hearing; you've heard them all before. A person may not even make sense. But the moment your eyes glaze over as if you're uninterested or don't care, conflict can erupt. So it's even more important to *look* interested than to *be* interested.

In Chapter 14 I dealt with the four levels of listening: Being open, literally hearing, interpreting, and acting. Underscore these by projecting a listening face.

EMPATHIZE

Let me clarify that while empathizing essentially means standing in the shoes of another or seeing through the eyes of another, I'm not suggesting you have to agree with that person. Obviously I didn't agree with the superstitious man who held his own son hostage and thought he had to blood-let him. But everyone is entitled to a point of view, right or wrong, just or unjust. Don't agree; just try to understand where the person is coming from.

Too many people confuse *empathy* with *sympathy*. You don't have to sympathize with or approve of another's actions or words. Just empathize and see how powerful it makes you. Don't do it to be nice; do it because it's the only way to hit upon a proper appeal.

There are four types of appeals you can make to people to try to get them to voluntarily comply with your wishes: the Ethical, the Reasonable, the Personal, and the Practical.

Empathizing will help determine which of these might be most effectively initially.

If you agree that as a contact professional, your work entails bending the will of others at times, you will also agree that the way in which you appeal to a person is key. Your reputation and power depends on how well you can skillfully manage other people's behavior.

The most powerful professional presence you can project is with a straight Ethical Appeal. The word *ethical* comes from the Greek *ethos,* meaning "self." In this case, it's your persona, your professional service face. Because of your role and carriage and bearing, this approach is seen and felt by others and forcefully establishes your credibility.

Think of the ethical appeal as your professional face as you present it and as it impacts upon another person. The ethical appeal is Step 1 in the Five-Step Hard Style (see Chapter 12): Ask. The way you ask somebody to do something, particularly tonally, establishes whether you want to help or are just there to cause a problem. If I asked a man, "Would you please step out of the vehicle?" I might get more cooperation than by barking at him to get out. My voice would indicate professionalism right from the start.

If people believe in you, in your service, in your desire to help, often that in itself is enough to generate voluntary compliance. The moment the people you're dealing with begin to think you don't like them, or that you're irritated, or you don't like what you're doing, you lose the ethical appeal.

Then you have to solicit reason by moving to what I call the Reasonable Appeal. Because people are not always logical, especially when under duress, I have a basic rule with this one: Never use it when people are upset. First calm them, then try logic. Remember, under pressure common sense is a most highly uncommon commodity.

When you're setting context in Step 2 of the Five-Step Hard Style, you are using the reasonable appeal. You're saying, "This is policy, this is procedure, these are the grounds I have to stand on, these are my constraints." This approach alone will calm many people.

With truly difficult people the third appeal, Personal Appeal, tends to be most powerful. Why? Because with this appeal you're putting what you want them to do in terms of what they have to gain or lose. Are most people selfish? You bet they are. So hook into their attention span. Very few people will go against their own interests, including me. This appeal has been used effectively on me numerous times, especially when I've been upset at people in positions of authority. When they show me how what they're doing will ultimately benefit me, they win me over. Very powerful.

The fourth appeal is a strange one I call the Practical Appeal. This involves the use of offbeat strategies—like humor, redirection, and refocusing—that will gain voluntary compliance, provided they do not compromise your safety or integrity or violate your organization's policies.

When faced with resistance, try varying your appeal, but always display empathy.

ASK

There is a process of asking questions that can make you more skillful. I never had much training in asking questions, and I doubt you have either. Most people have no idea that there are actually at least five different types of questions.

Fact-finding (who, what, when, where, why, and how)

Fact-finding questions ask for specific data. Most people are naturally pretty good at these because they often concern practical matters and require only clear-cut answers. But they don't often have the best effect on people.

General

By definition, general questions are open-ended, for example, "What really happened here today?" In reply, a person

can say anything he wants. This allows him to choose the
direction of his answer and makes him feel good.

Opinion-seeking

Like general questions, opinion-seeking questions ask for an
opinion and allow latitude. You might ask, "Is there some
way we can solve this problem? What's your view of how we
ought to go about this?"

This approach is very powerful, because most everyone
likes to voice his opinion. Even if you're not terribly interested
in the answer, ask anyway, and remember to look interested
and make it obvious that you're listening. You may be surprised. The person might even have something profitable
to say.

Direct

Direct questions are basically your yes and no questions. "Did
you dump the garbage on this man's lawn?" "Did you go to
so-and-so's house?" "Did you spend the money?"

Though the questions may not in themselves be antagonistic, too many direct questions in a row can make people
feel machine-gunned. I had a problem with this when I was
a new cop because I was more interested in getting information for my reports than I was in being empathetic with
those involved.

Leading

Leading questions almost always anger people because
essentially they put words into their mouths. "Isn't it true
that ... ?"

You need to be as strategic as possible in your questioning, and I recommend two tactics.

First, try setting context for people before launching into
your questions. I call it "forecasting." In other words, simply
explain the direction and purpose of your questioning. Don't

just start firing questions. Say, "Friend, I have six or seven questions here, mostly concerning the cause of your trouble. I wonder if you'd be willing to work with me and try to answer them?" If people don't know how many questions you have, what they're about, and that you're going to stop, they become impatient and tenser as you go on.

It's always appropriate to tell people what you're about. It calms them and makes them more cooperative, and that means the nature of the information you get will be far better.

Second, vary your questions. This also lessens resistance and calms an audience. Start with a series of general questions to loosen people up, then ask some opinion-seeking questions. Gradually, naturally, move to the more direct and fact-finding questions. Resort to leading questions only when necessary.

Of my five types of questions, the general and the opinion-seeking do more to generate voluntary compliance than the other three put together. They make you appear empathic, caring, open, and unbiased, whether or not you really are. Direct and leading questions anger people much of the time.

The moment you see in the eyes of someone that he is becoming tense, you know he's probably feeling attacked. That's the time to move right back to a general question. The ability to fasten down on somebody and to lighten up when necessary by varying your questions is one of the great arts of interrogation.

It's also one of the great arts of talking to your children. You know how far you get with the typical "How was school?" *Fine.* "Well, how was English?" *Fine.* Try some others of my five types of questions, especially with teenagers, or you may never extract information from them until they're adults.

PARAPHRASE

When someone comes at you with verbal abuse, forget the tone and the emotion. Put the complaint in your own words and play it back for him. Even if you've misunderstood, he can see that you're trying, and he'll want to help you get it straight (see Chapter 10 for my Fourteen Benefits of Paraphrasing, how to do it, and several examples).

SUMMARIZE

Summarizing is a different use of language altogether. By definition it means condensing, taking all that's been discussed and putting it into a simple, concise statement.

I've long been interested in why some people convey a sense of authority and decisiveness that others lack, and I think one of the clues lies in the way they summarize.

Summarizing must have three qualities. It must be *brief, concise,* and, above all, *inarguable.* Let's say as a police officer I stop five people fighting in the street and I listen, empathize, ask, and paraphrase, and finally it comes time for me to make a decision. That decision statement, that declaration of what my choice of action will be, must sound authoritative. People must know how serious I am by the way I go about making my statement.

I might say, "Okay, gentlemen, ladies, listen up! You, sir, are free to leave if you leave right now. You two, sir and ma'am, get in your car and head south. And you, sir, you head north. You weren't getting along when I came here and I want you heading in opposite directions before I leave. And, you, you're under arrest. Place your hands behind you. I'm arresting you for such and such under the penal code of the state of . . ."

Now, notice I've left no room for argument. Leaving the arrest until after sending the others packing makes clear that I know exactly what I'm talking about and that I will brook no more discussion. How I said it clarifies that discussion is over. Much of summarizing is effected in the voice. You must sound as if you have reached the end, and you are now, in your professional capacity, executing the conclusion of the matter. If you have preceded your summary with the first four tools in LEAPS, your audience will have been made much more receptive.

Another benefit of summarizing is that it can reconnect communication when it's been interrupted. Interruptions are one of the phenomena of modern-day communication. While you're conversing, the phone rings. Or someone else butts in. To simply turn back to the other person and pick up where you left off without any summarizing bridge is a mistake. By then the other person's mind has wandered. He's not anchored in the last word you said. Capsulizing where you are at that point will ensure that he once again becomes a good listener. This form of summarizing can take the form of something as simple as "Now, Jack, we were on the subject of your tardiness and you were telling me what you were going to do to remedy it. Is that right?"

The former head of Los Alamos National Labs once told a colleague and me, "Miscommunication is the sand in the gears of modern technology." We all make mistakes everyday, but listening, empathizing, asking, paraphrasing, and summarizing can go a long way to making you more effective.

22

Applying LEAPS to Your World

MOST NEW SUPERVISORS think they have to start talking, to dominate, to demonstrate their opinions. But this four-step approach can ensure greater communication effectiveness.

1. *Ask.* Ask your people what they feel, what they want, or how they think things are going.
2. *Listen actively.*
   (*Repeat Steps 1 and 2 as many times as necessary until you feel you have heard everything.*)
3. *Reevaluate your position.* Be sure of where you stand, based on your people's input. Don't change your mind unless that is the right and appropriate course. But don't be afraid to do that. Your people won't see you as weak and manipulable; they'll admire your strength.
4. *Deliver the information.* Get before your people and tell them how it is going to be. You're in charge. You're the boss, but you don't have to say that. The day you need to remind people who's the boss is the day you should realize you have lost your people.

Using the first three steps, you will be much more skillful.

You have discovered where the pockets of resistance are. You know what people are thinking. And you can say something like "Okay, ladies and gentlemen, yesterday I listened to you and I heard you. We agree on a great many issues, and I'm glad you told me about A, B, and C because I want to address those immediately. About D, E, and F, I don't have enough input or resources to handle them at this time, but I'm asking the following people to get back to me in three months to see where we stand on those important issues..."

You may not have changed a thing, but you know your audience better. You can couch information in their language and appear more competent and in touch.

These four steps can help you be a great supervisor if you can avoid the common trap of jumping in and delivering information.

The five great tools of communication in LEAPS can save you untold trouble and create for you credibility which other people can't destroy. You can feel good about what you're doing, avoid conflict, and raise your own estimation of your ability as a professional.

Others often base how they feel about you on how you communicate. As you master these skills, people will begin to admire you. Short of building a Charles Atlas body and beating up the bully who used to kick sand in your face at the beach, I can think of no other unequivocal method of achieving admiration than by mastering Verbal Judo.

DON'T THANK ME FOR SHOPPING HERE!

Maybe you've had an experience similar to mine. You go to a city or a county bureau with a problem. Maybe it's your tax bill or trouble with your water, whatever. But isn't it rare when you get the feeling that the people working there care about serving you? I mean, that's not only their job—their sole reason for being there—but it's also what our tax dollars are supposed to pay for.

I know those people are there eight to ten hours a day

and are listening to similar complaints all the time. But clearly no one has ever taught them to number one, keep their egos out of encounters with the public; number two, find the right words for the person they're talking to; and number three, serve people by empathizing with them. In other words, make my experience more pleasant by the way you serve me.

We shouldn't be surprised at these bureaucratic lapses, because even in a lot of our retail profit centers, where happy customers are repeat customers, we receive very little good personal service. That's why we tend to teach formulas to people like "Thank you for shopping here." (Sometimes I think I'm going to lose it if I hear that one more time.)

I know it's not the clerk's fault. He or she has been trained to parrot that phrase, just as waitresses and waiters have been told to say, "Enjoy," when they slide a thirty-dollar meal under your nose. Or, "I'm Stacy and I'll be your server." Please! I love the idea of getting the name, but does anyone think it makes me feel special when I get the same patter as everyone else?

I want to hear something unique or at least fresh that tells me they're really glad I'm giving them my business and they'd like to make me so happy that I'll not only come back, but that I will also recommend the place to my friends.

The reason we provide formulas for people is that we don't trust them to interact with the public. But certainly you, as I do, recognize a formula when you hear one. I hate them because I know I'm hearing the same thing everyone else has heard that day. I'm no longer an individual. I'm not really being made to feel special. I'm simply getting the canned phrase, the pasted-on smile, and the singsong farewell that everybody gets.

There's nothing more irritating than standing in a long line and hearing every shopper get the standard, "Thank you for shopping here. Have a nice day!" Sometimes as soon as it's my turn I beat the clerk to the punch. I say, "Whatever you do, don't thank me for shopping here!"

"But, but, sir, what's wrong?"

And I say, "Treat me like an individual. The woman who

just bought a bolt of silk and left the store ought to be thanked differently from me. We aren't the same people. She's a little old lady, obviously still industrious and independent. I'm a middle-aged man buying a shotgun and shells. How about a different message for each of us that shows that you care? The only thing we customers have in common is that we shop here and make you a profit and pay your salaries." In truth I want to shout, "What's the matter with you people?" but I know it's not the clerk's fault.

OF SILK AND SHOTGUNS

Clerks should be taught to be real, to be personal, to look for that unique aspect that gives direct contact to the customer. The little old woman who buys a bolt of silk could be genuinely thanked like this, "Hey, that's a beautiful color choice, ma'am. I hope you enjoy that. What are you making?" And after a brief interchange *then* thank the woman for buying it where she bought it, and remind her that she is guaranteed complete satisfaction.

And how about for me, the shotgun buyer? "That's one of the top brands we carry, sir. Looks like you're planning some serious hunting." You think I wouldn't love to talk about the trip I've got planned with my buddies? Then tell me you hope I got the service I required at the sporting goods counter and to feel free to call with any questions. *Then* thank me for shopping there. By that time, I'll be thanking you and meaning it.

But don't just say, "Thank you for shopping here" and leave it at that. Treat people like individuals.

23

Persuasion for Fun and Profit

DON'T EXPECT VOLUNTARY compliance just because you have a position of authority or responsibility. Generate it. Make it happen.

The top communicators—the great cops, leaders, administrators, and managers—know the art of putting things in such a way as to make people more cooperative. The old samurai used to say, "To know and to act are one and the same." To paraphrase Shakespeare, "Suit the word to the deed and the deed to the word." In other words, avoid the disastrous use of language best summed up in the old Chinese adage, "Control your emotion, or it will control you."

One of my favorite samurai maxims says, "The angry man will defeat himself in battle as well as in life." We live in the most dangerous of all eras. We are living closer together; there are people under the influence of drugs, liquor, rage, fear, anxiety, ignorance, and stupidity; and violence is commonplace. The key to our success—not to mention our survival—is our ability to stay calm and avoid the anger that makes us ineffective.

The anger that made me ineffective as a cop will also

make me ineffective as a businessman, an entrepreneur, a husband, a father, a boss, a seminar leader. As I've tried to make clear, I'm one of the original Difficult People. My first reaction to stress is to confront. Somebody crosses me, watch out. I'm ready to do battle. Fortunately or unfortunately, I'm well trained for physical encounters. I've learned the hard way, though, that winning a battle at the physical level means losing the war in every other respect.

I've finally learned, after years of teaching this stuff and seeing it work on the streets, that Verbal Judo is akin to fishing. I like to fish the high mountain streams and lakes, up to ten thousand feet above sea level. If I'm not skillful up there, I can't hook a thing. And if I do hook a fish, I don't just reel him in as one would a carp. I have to play him in. I play and reel, play and reel, play and reel. When I finally do land one, I get a great feeling of satisfaction and accomplishment. That's also how I feel when I've encountered Difficult People, people like me. Developing the *mushin* state of mind, that calm center, means regarding Difficult People as a challenge rather than as combative adversaries.

Doesn't it make sense that we should develop a mindset that allows us to interact with these people skillfully, rather than letting them get our goat? The samurai warrior, when surrounded by attackers, went absolutely still inside. He prepared himself by being still so he would not be caught by surprise. He could respond to an attack from any direction, no matter how unexpected.

Train yourself to be free of bias, prejudice, and expectation. That's easier said than done, of course, and I'm the first to admit that it isn't something that comes naturally. There is a Chinese word that means both "crisis" and "opportunity." By remembering that, I am now able to like Difficult People, or at least to appreciate where they're coming from and view them as challenges and opportunities rather than obstacles.

If a guy gets in my face and says, "I can't do this and I won't do that," I just laugh inside and think, *My kind of a guy.* These are the kinds of people that shaped America. They are people of savvy, of backbone, of principle, of will. Think about it: A whole day of Nice People would be boring, but a whole day of Difficult People makes us work. They draw on our skill, make us flex our Verbal Judo skills, and leave us feeling good about our encounters as we succeed. Let me recommend that you begin viewing the Difficult People in your orbit as chances to prove your mettle rather than as people to avoid. Difficult customers should be interesting and challenging.

Notice that Difficult People cross all color boundaries and cultural distinctions. The key to your survival is knowing the kind of person (Nice, Difficult, or Wimpy) you're dealing with, and it should make no difference whether a person is black, white, Hispanic, or Asian. I don't care if a person's a homosexual, a transvestite, or undecided. It's not my business. I care only what he's doing and my ability to redirect him for the better.

AVOIDING THE INNER VOICE

One of the ways to accomplish the task of redirecting behavior, keeping calm in the face of Difficult People, and gaining voluntary compliance is to remain sounding professional. That keeps you safe even when you may no longer care about safety. Inside, your voice may be saying what you really want to say. But one of the laws of effective communication is to never utter the inner voice. The inner voice is almost always negative. Control it at all costs and you'll find yourself way ahead of the game.

PERSONALIZATION

One of the last things our inner voice wants to do when encountering Difficult People is to give our name. Yet this gesture of personalizing the dispute, of showing no fear of being identified and being accountable for our decisions (and the policies of our governing body) is something that should be applied universally. I don't care whether you're a home-maker, a parent, a banker, an executive, a salesperson, or a service employee—you become more human when I know your name. And don't just offer it mechanically. It shouldn't be "Hi! I'm Stacey and I'll be your waitress." Slow it down. Give it some weight, some sincerity.

And how about something unique? Set yourself apart. Surely management doesn't expect you to be a robot, just like everyone else on the floor. The formulas they give you are principles, frameworks on which you should hang your own personality. I'd love it if a waitress would say something like "My name is Stacey Smith and it's my job to see that you leave here fat and sassy." Or "... it's my job to make sure you get everything you want to eat as quickly as I can get it for you." Later, when the check arrives, if the waitress has built appropriate rapport with me, I wouldn't mind a little humor. "It's also my responsibility to see that you don't leave without paying."

You see what I'm driving at? Something, anything that will humanize the encounter and make people feel as if they've been noticed and that they have mattered.

Nothing angers me more than when I call an agency and get a receptionist who gives me only a number. "This is two-four-four, sir. How may I help you?" I want to say that person can help me by telling me who I'm dealing with. I want a name. Names have a way of calming people. Names give you a sense that a human being is at the other end of the phone. How hard is it to say, "Good evening, sir, my name's George Thompson. What can I do for you?"? Even in a store, it helps if the clerk at the counter says, "Hi, I'm Beverly. Let me know if there's any way I can help you," rather than simply, "Can I help you?"

OUR REAL PURPOSE

Regardless of our profession or role, we're all in the business of meeting people's needs.

Consider your children. I've already talked about the fact that you have to decide between want and need and that if you gave kids everything they wanted you'd turn them into ugly, self-centered brats. But what about those real needs? Suppose you have a kid who needs a bicycle, but you don't have the money for the latest, high-tech model. Your job as a Verbal Judo practitioner is to convince him that a good used bike, for which he will pay half, will meet his needs and give him a great sense of accomplishment and satisfaction.

HOLSTERING YOUR DIVORCE WEAPON

Aren't divorce courts filled with people who've misunderstood this same point? You get angry at your spouse and draw down on him or her with the equivalent of a policeman's deadly force, perhaps with a sentence like "Well, if you don't like it, let's get a divorce!" And your spouse, equal to the challenge, responds, "Fine! See you in court!"

Soon there the two of you are, filing for something neither one of you really wanted. It makes no sense, but it's what happens when we fire from the hip, when we allow the words that come naturally to our lips make a speech we live to regret. Unless we're mighty in character and depth and know how to apologize, we wind up obligated to defend our ultimatums. Our pride, our face is at stake, and we will not back down. We end up making life-changing decisions to our own detriment. The only solution is to learn to ignore the inner voice and to use every Verbal Judo technique we know to keep us from doing irreparable damage to ourselves and our loved ones.

Give others a break too. Don't react to their words. A

spouse complaining about a wet towel on a bed or griping about your coming home late, or a boss snapping at you about some minor matter, are only symptoms of larger problems. Let the words go by, deflect them as I taught you earlier and set about addressing real issues.

24

The Misunderstood Motivator

No, I'M NOT referring to myself, though there are days when I feel misunderstood. The misunderstood motivator is Praise. When I'm praised correctly—and there are myriad incorrect ways to offer praise—I feel most understood and appreciated.

Have you ever felt suspicious when praised? You're not alone. I believe suspicion of praise is universal because it so frequently precedes criticism (which I will discuss). For example, "I really enjoyed your solo. It was beautiful. Now can I give you a few hints on your wardrobe and stage presence?" See how this compliment was yanked away like a rug from under the singer? This happens so often that when we hear a compliment we can't help but wait for the other shoe to drop.

Regardless, I contend that praise remains the most effective motivator and disciplinarian there is. Effective and genuine praise does far more than make people feel good. They tend to do voluntarily what they are praised for. But if they are criticized they will do just what they need to to get by.

Offering praise communicates and reinforces your values. And when praise is specific—as I will discuss more fully—it appears more authentic and increases your credibility, regardless of your role.

PRAISE AS PART OF YOUR ARSENAL

We know very little about praise, but it can be a dynamic tool. In my opinion, it is the single most powerful teaching weapon we have.

Praise has to be believable to work effectively, and people seem to feel as uneasy about praise as they do about criticism. They distrust it instinctively for they think criticism will follow, so praise has to be given with care.

My first praise principle is that if you plan to praise people, never follow it with criticism. If you do, from then on, whenever people hear a compliment from you (no matter how sincere), they will also hear in their minds, "... *but*..."

I'm not saying you cannot or should not criticize people when necessary. If you must, criticize first, then leave them with praise. You might tell an employee, "You know, I'm really upset about the way you handled that shipping problem yesterday afternoon. It did no good to blame the distribution staff, as overworked and underresourced as they are right now. You or someone you delegated should have simply apologized unconditionally to the customer and made sure the shipment went out immediately. That's the way you've been trained, and you have demonstrated that attitude many times. That's why you're in the position you're in. Though I want you to remember to respond the way you know is best in the future, I also want to tell you that your overall work has been exemplary. Specifically, your monthly reports are always right on the mark, giving me the information I need in a format that makes me look good when I pass them along. I know you can do that well in all areas, and I'm counting on you to do that."

I often ask my seminar students, "What is it that makes good praise?"

Almost invariably, they'll answer, "Sincerity."

That's close, but I say, "All right, how do we make praise sound sincere?"

One of the ways has to do with where you insert praise into the conversation: last, not first. Not first and last with a criticism sandwiched in between either. That's a popular management recommendation, but I think people see through that as easily as they see through the compliment-then-criticism technique. The employee misses the first bit of praise because he's been called on the carpet and is waiting for the other shoe to drop. Then he gets the bad news and he can't appreciate the other half of the sandwich cookie. Whatever came before the "but ... ." he no longer believes because it was an obvious setup. Whether it really was or not is irrelevant. If that's the way he feels, that's reality to him.

The second way to effect the sincerity of praise is to make it as specific as possible. There is something disconcerting about "Nice going! Good job! Appreciated that." It's much better when someone says—to use the singing example again—"I enjoyed your solo, especially the song you selected and the way you interpreted that chorus. I felt as if I were young and in love again."

I was the happy beneficiary of specific praise, and I'm pleased to say it helps bolster my point. To use one of my earlier phrases, I was an "unconscious competent" at public speaking. I have saved until now the news that I was a stutterer as a child because I believe it has more impact when you have established in your mind that I make my living by giving speeches hundreds of times a year.

When I was a student I couldn't get out sentences that began with words like *why, what,* or *how.* Basically, I couldn't ask any questions. This dogged me into my freshman year of college. I had to rephrase questions so they wouldn't start with a *w* or an *h* word. I had to say things like "Tell me about that. It seems that wouldn't work if this was the case." I didn't know it, but I was becoming more verbally fluent because of my weakness. If I put *what* in the middle of a sentence, I could get it out. So I began most of my questions with a dependent clause—which is not a bad way to pose a question. Still, I was insecure, and for years I didn't even consider teaching, let alone public speaking, as a career.

Yet as I gained confidence, I saw the stutter begin to disappear until finally I was a teacher, then a professor, and finally a public speaker. No one knew that I still harbored insecurities about my speaking ability because of those painful memories, so I took any praise for my oratory with a grain of salt. At times I was tempted to say, "I'm glad you enjoyed it, but if you only knew..."

In the mid-1980s I spoke to an audience of realtors in Chicago and learned a valuable lesson. Afterward, people filed out gushing general praise like "Great speech! Loved it! Best I've ever heard!"

As was my habit I pasted on a smile and responded with, "Thank you. Oh yes. Thanks. Oh yes. 'Preciate that."

The last guy to leave the room said, "I really enjoyed that," and I started in with one of the variations of my "Oh yes" when he got my attention. When he added, "...specifically," I cocked my ear.

He said, "Specifically I like the way you use little everyday stories to teach complex points like empathy and setting of context. Most speakers don't do that. Those stories made me see your points. Thanks for putting those in there." And he walked out.

THE BENEFITS OF SPECIFIC PRAISE

1. Specific praise feels good. It made me feel good. The specificity of his praise reached me as no general praise could have. Specific praise is powerful praise; general praise is just good manners.
2. Specific praise is believable. Because he had been spe-

cific, I believed him. He was credible and that made *him* look good too.

3. Specific praise always either reinforces or teaches. It made me learn something about myself as a speaker. In all honesty, I had not previously had a clue to my success. I knew I was in demand and that people seemed to appreciate and enjoy my speaking. But if I'd had to guess, I would have said it was because they liked my style. I'm expressive, hard-driving, and I don't do a lot of gyrating. I get to the point—it's just in-your-face principles and give 'em the bottom line.

   I have always been a storyteller, but until that guy pointed out that the specific detail of my illustrations made my points come alive for him, I didn't know. I might have drifted from that technique, but once I knew it was effective, I went back and emphasized stories and illustrations for all my presentations. His specific praise taught me to be a better speaker.

4. Specific praise gets passed along. Two years later I ran into a guy in Jacksonville, Florida, who said, "Are you that crazy guy from Albuquerque who teaches Verbal Judo? I've got a friend in Chicago who raved about your course. He couldn't remember your name but he never forgot what you did."

   I said, "What was that?"

   He said, "You taught with specific little stories the way Einstein taught physics. My friend had to give a presentation before his bosses and he completely redid it based on that one principle alone. And he gave the best speech."

It pays to listen and watch and take that extra time to look at what somebody does that makes you feel good. Then, instead of just blurting, "Great job!" be specific.

AN EXAMPLE

Let's say I have an employee—I'll call him John—who writes poorly. His reports are a mishmash of abstract generalities. I send him to a writing course, but he's not much better. I look through thirty of his reports and they're all bad. My natural inclination might be to take a handful of those reports and shake them in his face and say, "Didn't you learn anything? These are outrageous! If you don't get better, we'll fire you!"

Obviously, that would be ineffective. On the basis of my principles of praise, here's what I should do. I should take the time to dig through all those reports to find at least one paragraph that works. It might be just dumb luck on John's part, but something somewhere in that mass of writing has to be something worthwhile. Then, instead of trying to resort to criticism and an ultimatum as a motivator, I should try specific praise.

I should not call John in, but rather seek him out. I should say, "John, I was looking over some of your reports, and I was impressed with this paragraph and how specific it is. That's good, because when you're this specific, it helps me understand what you do so I can supervise you better. That's good for you. That's good for me. That's good for everybody. Thanks for taking the time to do that."

You think his next report wouldn't be fifteen times more specific? You can bet he'd go home and tell his wife that night that the boss had praised him, and there's little question that he'd remember why. People do what they're praised for. If I were to only criticize him, he would just shore up his reports just enough to keep me off his back. Criticized people generally do only enough to reach a level of what management experts call "minimal competency." That's what's wrong with labor in our society.

Now let's say John is doing better on his reports, but he's

still neglecting to open and close them with power and influential statements. Now I can go to him and say, "John, your reports are more specific than ever, and I appreciate it. And this one opened with a powerful, grabbing sentence. Open and close the rest of them that way, and you're writing the best reports we can get. I know you can do it."

A QUIZ

Beside exercising the principle of specific praise, what other Verbal Judo principle am I using?

If you said I was raising John's expectations as a way to motivate him, you're among the best readers I've got. If you keep catching on to these principles and remembering them ... well, you get the point.

Motivate by raising expectations. Raise expectations not through criticism, but through praise. Praise specifically, and you will find yourself resorting to criticism rarely.

CRITICISM WITHOUT OSTRACISM

You can, and many times should, deliver criticism effectively, directly, and even bluntly. As the flip side of the praise principle, the trick here is to follow the criticism—not precede it—with praise. That way, despite his mistakes, the person being corrected and criticized will still feel a part of the team, a valued player. If praise is doled out before criticism, as is usually the case, the person will feel manipulated. Often it's appropriate to remind the person, "If I didn't value you and care about you, or if I wasn't concerned with how you fit into the organization, I wouldn't bother to deal with you about this problem. If you were on your way out of the company or I thought you were unsalvageable, I wouldn't waste my time, would I? Do football coaches holler at marginal players?

No. They push and prod the ones they count on and need the most."

WHEN *YOU* ARE CRITICIZED

I have just a few simple guidelines for taking criticism, which we all must at times. None of these will be new to you, but it is worthwhile to list them here as reminders.

1. Maintain eye contact. Don't roll your eyes as if you are amazed at the stupidity of the person doing the criticizing. And don't cast your eyes down either. That is a sign of resignation or defeat. The person criticizing you probably doesn't want you to wallow in self-pity. Take it like an adult. Look the person in the eye and indicate that you're listening.

2. If you disagree, hold your tongue for the time being. If you constantly interrupt to correct an inaccuracy or plead your case, you're going to look worse. Maybe you're right and the criticizer is wrong. Still, arguing and appearing defensive will only make the person believe more strongly that he is right. The time may come when it is appropriate to defend yourself, but gather your thoughts first and be prepared to discuss them calmly, just to try to balance the record.

3. Nod and show an open body language that says you're not only listening, but also that you're hearing and understanding. You're not necessarily agreeing, but you're getting the message.

4. Use phrases that confirm your openness to be corrected such as "Uh-huh," "Yes," "Okay," "I hear you," "I understand what you're saying," "I'm willing," "I'll make every effort," "I'll work on that," "Thanks for pointing that out."

5. When you have the floor, use the opportunity not only to defend yourself but also to reiterate that you welcome such input and want to learn. Insist on a

follow-up meeting with a request such as "Could I check back with you to make sure I'm making progress and doing what you want?"

Being criticized and responding appropriately can be better than never having been noticed at all. Your demeanor and ability to choose your words carefully make all the difference.

25

You Can Punish Without Drawing Blood

As PARENTS WE sometimes have to punish our children. As employers, we sometimes have to punish employees. You may dislike doing this or even the idea of it, but you can't deny the reality: The ability to punish effectively is a necessary skill.

It's been my experience and observation that in our society we do not wield the sword of authority with great skill. That has led me to develop what I call the "principle of punishment." It goes like this: Though there are many ways to punish, when doing so you must use language without bias. In other words, never mix emotion and punishment.

I realize this is a whole lot easier said than done, especially with children. Parents are in all probability lying if they say they have never punished in anger. That's why cops deal with so much child abuse and domestic violence. We all know better, but knowing and doing are too often two different things. A few hints may help you maintain the gap between emotion (or feeling) and handing down punishment.

KEEP IN MIND

If you're so angry at someone that you simply must express it, do so. But be careful not to effect punishment at the same time. Let's say you overhear your son speaking disrespectfully and totally inappropriately to your wife. It makes you mad, and you know he would benefit from knowing that. It's not all bad to light into him, but force yourself not to get into pronouncing a sentence until you're calmer.

In other words, you might raise your voice so he knows you're serious. You might say, "Listen, son, I'm not going to stand for your talking to your mother that way. It's disrespectful and it's going to stop or you and I are going to have trouble. Remember, that's not just your mother you're talking to—she's also my wife."

That will often get a raised eyebrow, but better yet, you have not followed your instinct to threaten what that trouble might be. You haven't flown off the handle and said you were going to knock his block off or ground him for a month or take away his driving privileges. That is something you want to avoid, because in the heat of the moment you may make one of those famous speeches you'll live to regret. You'll hand down a sentence that will be hard to enforce and probably be as much of an inconvenience for you and your wife as for your son.

If you have to chew out an employee, do it. But don't, in the excitement of the moment, say, "You're finished in this company. I'd fire you if I could. You're on probation for six months. No raise for you, etc., etc., etc." You might say to the employee, as you might say to your son, "I want to discuss this with you tomorrow to determine what we're going to do about it."

In the meantime, you will have a better handle on what really went wrong, how purposeful the infraction might have been, how serious the consequences, and what the most remedial and effective punishment would be. Anything decided in the fire of the moment will likely be counterproductive, cost the guilty party his face and dignity, and wind up being a burden for you.

The moment you use words that indicate you have lost respect for someone or don't like him, he shuts down and quits listening. Your personal self has intruded and spoiled your professionalism.

HOME SCHOOL

I learned a lesson with my son, Taylor, when he was six years old. I told him one day, "Don't throw the football in the living room because that vase over there came from Beijing, China, and was given to me by an old kung fu master. If you break that vase, you're history because that thing's irreplaceable, and by the way, my friend, you are not!" Now, obviously, I was teasing him and he knew it, but he also knew I was quite serious about the value of the vase and the import of my prohibition.

Two weeks later at three in the afternoon I heard a tremendous crash in the living room and knew immediately what had happened. I hurried in to find Taylor and the football and the vase, in pieces. I was so angry that I worried what I might do or say to him, and somehow I was able to control myself. I simply said, "You and I had a contract. No football in the living room. Go to your room and I'll see you in the morning."

Then I went out to the driveway where I had a hanging bag, and I beat that bag until my hands bled. I took my feelings out on the bag, not on the boy.

Suppose I had not done that. Suppose I had done what I had too often with my daughter. What if I had let my anger overwhelm me and said the first thing that came to mind? I would have begun lying. I would have said, "You SOB!" That's lie number one. "You never listen!" Lie number two. "You never do what I say!" Lie number three.

Then when I sent him to his room I would be pronouncing the same punishment, but I would have a different kid behind the door. I would have had a little boy steeped in righteous resentment for sixteen hours. He would have been crying, rocking back and forth, thinking *I am* not *an SOB. I do* too *listen. I do* too *do what he says. He's so unfair, blah, blah, blah.* Sixteen hours later he would come out worse than he was when he went in.

It's easy to snap and use Verbal Karate, to lash out and hurt someone with a wound that will never go away. Think of the long-term effect. How many times can we snap at our children that way and not turn them into mean, nasty street lizards who hate authority, hate cops, hate anyone in control? What will prevent them from turning to gangs for solace?

THE GOAL

I've established that the worst abuse in this world is verbal. So, if you want to be an effective punisher, you must learn to use language disinterestedly, unemotionally, and without bias. The goal of punishment should be positive. It is not to inflict pain or exact revenge. Rather it is to reconstruct, to make better, to educate.

If we agree that remediation and rehabilitation is the goal of effective punishment, why is the language associated with it usually so negative? Why do we feel the need to put people down when we punish them?

Don't think that I am unaware how difficult this lesson is. Only a fool would tell you that it's easy to control yourself when you're angry. But it can be done. And it's crucial to your effectiveness in punishing and to the well-being of both the person you're punishing and you. Stopping and silently counting to ten or twenty sounds like an old cliché, but it's not a bad idea if it works.

Train yourself to do the opposite of what you feel. If you feel like shouting, whisper. If you feel like striking, caress. If you feel like storming from the room, stay put. Take control. Feel the power it gives you. Above all, separate emotion from punishment.

26

Dancing When You Might Have Stumbled

HERE I WANT to celebrate the mastery of Verbal Judo. Many who have incorporated the various principles in their lives have elegantly succeeded in situations where once they might have suffered loss or embarrassment. You can succeed too if you're committed to following through on what you have learned.

I was one who suffered as much as anyone for lack of having discovered and mastered these principles. The failure of my marriages was largely due to the fact that no one had ever told me to not express my feelings when I got angry. Rather than saying, "I love you, what's wrong?" I said things like "If you don't like it, too bad. You want a divorce? Okay!"

We all find it hard, especially men, to say what we really feel and mean, and so we resort to shortcuts. We translate disappointment into anger, we translate frustration into anger, because it's easier for us to look good, macho, and powerful if we lash back.

Just as in the workplace, when you come home you must play a series of roles. You're a parent, a disciplinarian, a lover, a helper, a friend, a psychologist, or whatever is necessary at a given moment. I would take abuse and deflect it on the street, but then at home I wanted to relax. I dropped all pretense of skill at this, and my wife would say, "How come you don't treat me as well as you treat those street lizards you deal with? You're snapping at me like I'm a dog." She was right. Eventually it cost me the marriage.

In a later relationship, after I had begun developing this program but before I had mastered the ninja skill of making skillful communication invisible, my wife would say, "Don't use that Verbal Judo crap on me."

You're going to make mistakes. You're going to stumble. But it's better to stumble using the right technique with good motives. As important as learning these principles is making Verbal Judo part of the fabric of your life and character and personality.

Every time you interact with somebody in your family, on the street, or in your workplace, make it your goal to improve the situation or the relationship. If you try to control people, you'll be breathing down their necks. You can't force people to do what you want in today's society. You have to use your words strategically. Generate voluntary compliance and cooperation by directing rather than controlling.

GO AHEAD, MAKE MY DAY!

If you know movies, you know that famous Clint Eastwood line from the Dirty Harry series. He says to a punk, in effect, "Give me a reason to blow your head off." I gotta tell you, I love Clint Eastwood and all his Westerns and cop movies. But I bring that up in classes with real cops and I have to say, "There, for example, is the difference between TV and life. In the real world, you point a gun at a guy and say that, he reaches for the gun, and you shoot him—you're in deep trouble. In court it would be shown that you invited him to reach for a weapon so you could exterminate him, and you would be tried as a murderer."

Clint's approach may make for good theater, and we

may all cheer when Dirty Harry exacts justice from the sleaze ball, but that's the opposite of Verbal Judo.

When what we say or do forces someone to respond under duress, to whom are we giving the power to control the situation? To whom are we handing over the decision-making power? The badge wearer is the one who is supposed to make the *citizen's* day. The proper approach is: "I'll make your day for you. You want to resist arrest? You will not succeed. You want to fight a cop? You'll be subdued before you begin. You want to rape this woman or sell crack cocaine on these corners? I'm not going to let that happen."

RODNEY KING

Irrespective of your opinion of the verdict that resulted in the Los Angeles riots, a major question was brought to light by the Rodney King arrest. I happen to be one who believes the situation got out of hand and that entirely too much force was used. I believe in the justice system and the integrity of juries, and I have my questions about why King didn't simply obey and go immediately to a nonthreatening prone position. I know he was a repeat offender and was a large and dangerous man, but I have eyes as you do. I saw the videotape and was repulsed.

More important, though, for the first time in America a question was raised: What if the police, the thin blue line between peace and disharmony in our society, are the problem? That was something we didn't want to think about and, for the most part, had never considered. Charges of police brutality were few and far between and were often brought by obviously guilty parties. But when people who have long doubted those in power now start to wonder about the police themselves, we face a chilling question. Why should anybody trust the police to begin with?

I say to cops in my classes, "If out of the three hundred in this room there's just one of you suckers who thinks that showing up and kicking ass and taking names and humiliating people is what your job is about, what happens to the thin blue line between order and disorder, between peace and violence? It's gone."

That's the tragedy of the Rodney King affair. A lot of people say that it was business as usual in L.A., and of course a lot of L.A. cops say, "No, it isn't."

To me, the saddest part was that when it happened I was in the midst of a contract with the Los Angeles Police Department to teach Verbal Judo to most of its officers. Several of the cops involved in that ugly altercation were scheduled to sit in on one of my seminars the very next week. I like to think that something they might have gleaned from that would have put a different spin on what happened that night.

I can only hope that they would have danced rather than stumbled, because regardless whether anyone ever proves that anything they did that night was illegal, anybody with a brain and two eyes knows that the situation could have been handled better.

I want you to be able to dance instead of stumble, as I have learned to do, and I offer here a couple of case histories to show what kinds of results you might expect. Both involve people who have attended my seminars and have used the Verbal Judo techniques to great avail. While each has many stories of success in everyday dealings and negotiations, both have also soared on paper as little Davids doing written battle—one with a Goliath corporation and the other with a high-powered businessman. Both the corporation and the businessman tried to intimidate my protégés and might have scared off someone who had no ammunition, but you will see that Verbal Judo made my guys equal to the task in both cases.

THE WATER SYSTEM FROM HELL

My client, whom I'll call Rick, and his wife needed a water-softening system and a drinking water purifier. They sched-

uled a meeting with a sales representative from a supplier,
but the man who arrived was not the salesman. Rather, he
said he was a sales manager in an executive position who had
been forced to handle the house call because the route salesperson had had to cancel at the last minute because of a social
engagement.

This sales manager acted rushed and perturbed that he
had to handle such a lowly task but assured Rick and his wife
that they would be the beneficiaries of the snafu. He had a
personal vendetta against the salesman and would thus sell
both the softener and the purifier at cost. That would result
in no commission for the salesman, and the sales manager
said he would use the sale as a case lesson for his staff. He
bragged that this would prove to his staff that he could sell
the company's products under any circumstances.

He breezed through his presentation, apparently eager
to get going, and was unable to produce documentation for
his company's claims of research showing that their system
would eliminate the need for hair conditioners and fabric
softeners, reduce the need for soap, produce a no-
maintenance bathroom, and cut water bills to the bone. He
used to carry such documentation, he said, when he handled
house calls.

Rick and his wife expressed their reluctance at getting
into the middle of an office-politics situation, but they could
not ignore the huge price break. They had no reason to doubt
the sales manager's word about the research studies and the
water bill savings, so they signed the contract. The sales manager stayed long enough only to gloat again about how he
would use the deal to show his people how sales should be
done, even in difficult circumstances.

When the system was installed it seemed to run for several hours, water gushing down the drains. Rick called to see
if this was normal and was told a serviceman would come
that night. No one came. Reddish beads turned up in tap
water, toilets, sinks, and tubs. The next day Rick turned on
the shower, only to be blasted with the little beads he even-

tually learned were from the resin system designed to infiltrate the system.

When a serviceman finally came to check, Rick learned that the system had indeed malfunctioned and had dumped its entire tank of resin beads into the water supply. As Rick had ingested some of these in his shower, he was naturally concerned with his health.

But that was not all. Clearly the installer had been inexperienced. He left a mess, including a gaping hole in the drywall. He left greasy tools on a piece of Rick's luggage. The washing machine became so clogged with resin that the pump had to be replaced. The water heater had heavy residue from the beads.

Meanwhile, the system continued to malfunction. It would come on in the middle of the morning and shake the whole house, and the family noticed no savings in soap or conditioners. Their water bill increased sixfold!

When it became clear to Rick that the entire system was a disaster, he contacted the company, only to discover that the "sales manager" had misrepresented himself and had since been reassigned. Rick believed he was getting satisfaction when the company agreed to replace the system, promised to send documentation that his health would not be threatened by his resin shower, and urged him to try out the system (which would be fully explained at a later date) before paying anything.

Part of the original sales plan had included regular deliveries of salt. None came. The documentation regarding health-related issues and the chemistry of the resin was never sent. Rick did not receive any printed material or explanation of the system that would have told him what was normal and what was not, how the system best functioned, and what to expect.

What he and his wife did receive next was their bill, which had been turned over to a collection agency and was soon to be litigated.

I don't know about you, but I would have been ready to go to war. Phrases like "How dare you?" and "Who do you think you're dealing with?" would have come to my mind.

To Rick's credit, while he was forthright and unequivocal in his letter, he did much more than simply recount the history of the case (which is always a good idea). He could have ranted and raved and made all manner of threats and accusations. Rather, he clearly stated his personal offense at having been contacted by a collection agency and having been threatened with legal action when it was clear to him that it was he who had the case against the supplier. Instead of leveling a written version of "See you in court," he outlined how he thought he had been shortchanged, asked for restitution, and insisted on the company calling off the collection agency, using variations of the following language: "I await your earliest response. In view of our desire to avoid a court case—a feeling I assume would be shared by you and your company—I would ask that . . . " Later he added, "I trust we can work things out smoothly and professionally . . . "

In subsequent correspondence, when this approach seemed to be working, Rick looked for other areas of agreement. He wrote such things as "I feel you have taken some good initial steps in helping to alleviate the serious problems I outlined in my letter . . . My meeting with _____was cordial and he proved to be a fine tribute to your office."

While Rick continued to fear for his health, he even allowed, "I am neither a chemist nor a doctor, and do not want to suggest that the pains are linked to my ingestion of the resin beads. However, I would like to close the door to that possibility, and I will be able to do that by receiving the above-mentioned data from you."

He continued, "With that in mind, I would ask that you take additional action and waive all charges on this transaction. I challenge every dollar of this account." And then Rick concluded with what I often encourage as a solid Verbal Judo technique. He painted a word picture that allowed his target audience to envision exactly what was going on:

"I feel not unlike a gentleman farmer who buys what he thinks is a prize cow but is shipped a raging bull. After the buyer has been gored, some immediate concessions are made by the seller. The shirt with its gaping hole will be replaced and all cosmetic repairs will be covered at no cost. Bull food for a year will also be covered. But then the farmer is slipped a bill for the bull itself.

"Sir, I am grateful for the bull food. But can you do something about the bull? Please take another look at the figures and previous correspondence. I'd be appreciative if we could come to a meeting of the minds by the end of the year."

Best of all, once the matter was finally settled to Rick's satisfaction, he followed up with a note of thanks. It would have been easy to shoot a stinger back, gloating about the victory. But the company had eventually done the right thing, and Rick wrote:

"Thank you again for your assistance in resolving these matters. We are well aware that in any business, problems occur. What sets companies apart is how such problems are dealt with. Despite advertising claims about service, too often the customer loses. And so we have been encouraged to see our case handled in such a forthright manner. The professionalism displayed by you and your assistant has been refreshing indeed."

MANO A MANO

The other success story from one of my satisfied students (I'll call him Chris) is this: Chris, a businessman, ran into a real buzz saw in the person of a businessman who apparently used intimidation as a common negotiating tactic. Chris had simply requested business references from him, standard practice when you're about to enter into an agreement with someone.

He wrote the man, whom I'll call Frank, "I was able to reach two of the business references your office provided, but they weren't of much help. The first wouldn't take my call or call me back; the second gave me a minute to ask a couple of questions, and then offered to negotiate the deal if I needed help. The only help I need is for somebody to stand up and say, 'Frank's a great guy. He cuts a fair deal and I'd gladly do business with him again.' Please let me know if you can provide any references that will assure me. It's a fair thing to ask."

He then clearly challenged Frank's unfair-deal terms, stating, "These are basic questions that perhaps you'd prefer were left unasked, but not asking them would be an irresponsibility on my part..."

Chris expressed his willingness to meet face-to-face but added, "However, perhaps it's fortuitous that we haven't met, in light of your earlier threat, 'Don't mess with me, I'm Sicilian.' Or maybe it wasn't a threat. I honestly have trouble differentiating between what you say and reality as I know it."

(I gotta tell you, if that happened to me, I would have to be reminded to stay in my Verbal Judo mode to keep from placing a few calls to my friends and having fifty thousand cops land on Frank's doorstep. In this case, the student handled it better than the teacher would have.)

In the letter, Chris then moved to humor, in an attempt to counterbalance Frank's sweeping denigration of a group of people. "Either way, I can assure you that I don't want to wake up with a horse's head in my bed, if that's what you mean."

He concluded: "All of this is to say, Frank, I think it would be prudent to start trying to mend fences. And I think your attorney would advise the same if you gave him a copy of this letter. We're all pretty decent people on the other ends of these telephone lines. We also have solid reputations, simple values, a distaste for being 'messed with' which we apparently share with Sicilians, and wouldn't you know it—even a readiness to grab hold of an olive branch...if there's one anywhere in sight."

That letter, because of its tone and its expert use of Verbal Judo techniques, took Chris from an acrimonious situation to harmony overnight. One day he was receiving threats and charges and ultimatums from Frank's insisting that he would not do business with anyone if Chris was involved to his telling Chris that Chris's clients would go broke when Frank sued them. The next day after that letter arrived in Frank's mailbox—whether he showed it to his lawyer Chris isn't sure—he called Chris with a laugh in his voice. The tension was gone. He even offered Chris a writing job, telling him he had no idea Chris could put words together on paper like that! They got together for lunch, continued negotiating, and eventually inked a lucrative deal for all parties.

FROM ALL WALKS OF LIFE

My memory is full of testimonials from seminar attendees who have borne witness to the benefits of Verbal Judo. I hear from them all the time. There's the woman from Southern California who was sent to the seminar by her employer and who saw a huge decrease in complaints about her department. But even more important, she believes Verbal Judo saved her marriage. She began talking to her husband the way she wanted to be spoken to by him. He was surprised, bemused, and suspicious at first, but as she stuck with it, he grew to like it. Her ego was in the background. She was practicing the Golden Rule.

Eventually he felt conspicuous being the bad guy in a marriage with such a wonderful, loving wife, and his behavior began to change. She says she has taught him to be a Verbal Judo expert without his even being aware of it.

I've heard from cops who had been estranged from their kids, either because of divorce or separation or just because of the demands of the job. With Verbal Judo techniques they were able to say things they had never been able to say before, and they've seen friendships formed and relationships healed. They think it's magic and that I'm some sort of a family-healing guru.

But Verbal Judo is just common sense. I admit I have the right background for this type of a thing. I needed Verbal Judo myself, being a Difficult Person. I became a student of rhetoric and literature. I overcame a speech handicap. I worked in the trenches, where you have to be able to communicate to stay alive. And I perfected physical martial arts skills which I found transferred beautifully to this program.

Yet I maintain there is no magic to it, no deep secrets. Learn the principles so that even when the myriad techniques don't come immediately to mind, you'll know the general objective.

Make Verbal Judo a way of life, and watch yours change for the better.

27

Verbal Judo as an Automatic Response

My GOAL IN this chapter is to present to you twenty-six of the most compelling ideas I have gleaned from the streets. As I have emphasized, just about anything that works in the crucible of the street can be adapted and transferred to everyday life.

I have a list of maxims and credos I call Secret Power Samurai. If you take the time to think these through and memorize them, they will spring to mind when you're in a crisis. Consider this a refresher course on much of what has gone before, reminders of the phrases that will allow you, under pressure, to marshal your communication strength in ways that might surprise you.

Some of these may seem clear and obvious, while others may amaze you, but each can markedly contribute to your ability to become a fine verbal communicator.

These principles will help you affirm the truth of the famous Sun-tzu, who once said: "To win a hundred victories in a hundred battles is not the highest skill; to subdue the enemy without fighting, that is the highest skill."

A more modern martial arts figure, the late Bruce Lee,

211

said it this way: "You and your opponent are one." In other words, you coexist and you become his complement, absorbing his attack and using his force to overcome him.

If you have gained nothing else from this book, remember that the principle of Verbal Judo is the same as that of physical judo. Instead of pushing back and confronting, you want to redirect, using the energy of the other. According to Sun-tzu and Lee, two famous fighters, two thousand years of encounters have taught us that the most powerful warriors are people who do not engage in physical conflict.

Power is knowledge in action. If you put to work the knowledge contained in this book, you will develop the power to stay calm and to achieve self-esteem when others expect you to stumble. That is the subtle power to get what you want without being obvious about it. If your technique is too obvious, people sense you are trying to manipulate them, and you'll fail for sure.

The man who has mastered an art reveals it in his every action. I've lived Verbal Judo now for nearly two decades. I learned it slowly, made a lot of mistakes, and have the physical and emotional scars to prove it. That's why I want you to take these maxims seriously, so that every time you interact with people you can put them into effect. Your goal should be to make Verbal Judo a natural response, something in your character that reveals itself to your children, to the plumber who tries to hand you a bill you think is too high, to the contractor who is taking longer than you think he ought, or to the supervisor you think is unfair.

Use the skills represented by these maxims to redirect behavior rather than getting into an ugly confrontation. If the thought of memorizing all of them overwhelms you, select five favorites and try to put them into action tomorrow. Use them with your family, your peers, your colleagues, your public.

THE PRINCIPLES OF IMPARTIALITY

The twins of great communication are the same great twins
of police work:

1. Always maintain your professional face; never strive
   to save your personal face. Your personal face is ego
   on your sleeve, your expression of irritation, anger,
   and bias. I would have paid somebody to teach me
   that principle when I was twenty-one.
2. Always treat the other person as you would want to
   be treated under identical circumstances. This is
   really the Golden Rule, isn't it? It's in the Bible and
   we've heard it all our lives, but how many of us live
   it out? The next time your children misbehave, treat
   them as you wish you had been treated when you
   were that age. Too often people grow up and become just like the parents they resented. That's why
   child abuse is perpetuated through the generations.
   These twin principles of communication are easy to
   recite but hard to implement. Most of the mistakes
   I've made can be traced directly to my failure to
   follow them. I've either allowed my personal face to
   come through or I have failed to even think of the
   Golden Rule.

MORE ON MY LIST

3. Be careful to distinguish between reasonable and
   severe resistance. Reasonable resistance is any kind
   of verbal resistance you encounter that does not in-
   terfere with your ability to complete your job. When
   you think about it, it is fairly common. Let it go.
   Ignore it. Don't let it annoy or distract you. It ties
   in with my reminder to let a person say what he
   wants as long as he does what you say.

People have different tolerance levels. How much can you take and not get upset? I urge you, if you want to be successful, to increase the quotient. Work on increasing your resistance level so you can keep from *reacting* and emphasize *responding* (see principle 9).

Admittedly, there are times when you will face what I call severe resistance, a level of resistance that markedly interferes with your ability to get your job done. That is the time to draw the line, to deal with it and get your adversary back in line.

4. Every verbal encounter is unique. You may work with the public all day and communication may seem to you like a stream of endless repetition. If you're ineffective, it may be because you have bought into that myth. As a cop, I learned that my life depended on my ability to see each car stop as unique. With twenty or thirty stops every eight hours, I had to remember that each of itself was different, no matter how routine it might have looked. In the workplace, remember that your customers don't realize they are asking you the same question you have been asked a dozen times already. To each the question is important. The forty-first person who calls does not want to be treated as if he had called forty times earlier.

Make that forty-first caller feel as if he were your first or only call of the day. Empathize!

5. As a contact professional, you alone have the responsibility to create and maintain continuous rapport with people. Verbal Judo is a hands-on art. Don't expect others to become pleasant, malleable, or compliant.

6. Always check your own assumptions. Your assumptions may be wrong. Be aware of your influence. For example, I answered a call about a loud party once, took a lot of verbal abuse, and had to be forthright to get them to turn down the volume. Forty minutes

later I was called back again, this time naturally assuming that I would be treated the same way. I approached the scene with more vigor and negativity, only to be surprised that they were much more compliant this time, and we were able to settle the matter for good. I was fortunate I didn't make the situation worse by allowing my logical, but false, assumption to make me act inappropriately.

7. Control encounters; don't become a victim of them. Think of yourself as a contact professional who, from the beginning, will control the situation. Don't let people foot-sweep you by getting you upset.

    If you can't control yourself, you can't control the situation. It starts with you. You have to be in control to create control.

8. Use adrenaline; never be ruled by it. A professional fighter with blood pouring from his mouth and nose can nevertheless manage a fine left uppercut and knock his opponent to the canvas. He has used his adrenaline to his advantage, and now it is raging. But he doesn't jump on his opponent and risk losing the fight by hitting a man while he's down. He goes to a neutral corner, because that's the law of the ring.

    As people hassle you and put pressure on you, take pride in your role and think like Michael Jordan: The more others pour it on, the better you should play.

9. Respond to people; never react. The word *respond* comes from the Latin *respondere,* meaning "to reanswer." The word *react* suggests that you're being controlled from the outside.

    When you are responding, you are in control. You are reanswering, responding to the event with power. When, on the other hand, you react, the event is controlling you.

    Hamlet said, "The readiness is all." Be ready to respond, no matter what. Even if someone is suddenly in your face, accusing you of something you had not even imagined possible, don't react, don't fly off the handle and say things you'll wish you hadn't.

10. Flexibility equals strength; rigidity equals weakness. This is a principle of the ancient samurai, who spent years teaching young warriors flexibility. The rigid mind breaks under pressure. You want to be like the willow tree that bends in the heaviest windstorm but does not break.

   If you are a head-up, face-forward, marching kind of a person, you're going to fail at home, in business, and in life. Take pride in your ability to bend and flex, looking for voluntary compliance, working toward better communication.

11. Avoid the depersonalization of abstraction. Keep your language specific. Abstraction has a killing quality. Airlines, for example, too often refer to passengers as fares. The U.S. government managed to depersonalize the Vietnam war for many years by referring to the dead as casualties, VC, or GIs. We didn't lose any George Thompsons or John Smiths. We lost a Vietcong or a Government Issue, which, like a rifle or a blanket, is inventory, no longer a person.

   I recommend addressing older people by their last names. "Excuse me, sir, your last name again? Mr. Johnson? Mr. Johnson, I have a question..." If you're talking to a younger man, I recommend using his first name. "Excuse me, sir. May I call you Jim? Jim, I'm curious about..." That specificity suggests that you care.

   Abstract depersonalization is destroying our society. Don't let your children label a person racially, instead of as an individual, or they will never be able to skillfully or successfully interact with those different from themselves. Teach them the power and dignity of specificity and personalization.

12. Use positive feedback when you least feel like it. It's easy to be positive with someone you feel good about. There's real skill in being positive when what you feel is negative.

One busy Saturday night I responded to a call about an underaged kid in a bar. He gave me a lot of trouble and it took me ten minutes to talk him out of there. It was a dangerous place, so I played it smart, not getting rough and causing a disturbance. When he finally walked out the front door he said sarcastically, "All right, Officer. I'm out of the bar now."

It was all I could do to not say what I felt. I wanted to threaten him and throw him in the squad car, but I was testing this very principle. I forced myself to realize that I had gained some voluntary compliance, sarcastic as he was. Did he come out? Yes. Was his attitude bad? Yes. Is that unusual? No. I decided to emphasize the positive and see what happened.

I said, "Let me tell you something..." and I could see him getting ready for some negative feedback. But I said instead, "I really appreciate your coming out. It's a busy Saturday night and I've got better things to do than to get into a tussle with you. And you must have something better to do than get into a tussle with the police and go to jail. Look, we're talking about a minor report. What do you say we skate on over to that patrol car a half a block away, get this juvenile summons done, and you're on your way. No big deal. What do you say?"

You should have seen the look on that guy's face. He said okay, and I was gone in five minutes, paperwork done, back to serve the public.

If I had emphasized the negative and gone with my instincts, it could have resulted in chaos, a fight, backups called, lots of paperwork, and time out of service. As it was, I got maximum effectiveness with minimum effort.

Try that with the people in your orbit. Do the unexpected. If they expect you to be negative, be positive.

13. Use self-talk to maintain control when under assault. Remember your acronyms:
    PAVPO: *P*erspective, *A*udience, *V*oice, *P*urpose, *O*rganization—the overview of rhetorical perspective.
    PACE: *P*roblem, *A*udience, *C*onstraints, *E*thical presence—the way to read a scene.
    LEAPS: *L*isten, *E*mpathize, *A*sk, *P*araphrase, *S*ummarize—the five great tools of communication.

14. Never violate the equity principle. Treat people equally, regardless of their age, race, appearance, or apparent value to you.

15. Cultivate your constituency; don't try to run people's lives. If a customer or an employee is difficult, for example, try going the extra mile for him. He's not expecting that, and he will never forget it. Every time you touch somebody with words you have an opportunity to make him feel better about his relationship with you. That gives you ultimate power.

FOR THE TOUGHEST CASES

Many of the rest of these principles are from the ancient samurai, some from my street experience, and all have been tested in the Verbal Judo laboratory of real life. They relate more to situations that have escalated to an emotional pitch and have the potential to turn ugly.

16. It's not enough to be good; you've got to look good and sound good or it's no good. To make that easier to remember, you might cast it in shorthand the way the ancient samurai may have said it: "Not enough to be good; got to look good or no good."

In today's society it's no longer enough to simply do the right thing. There are too many video cameras, too many tape recorders, and too many people who will sue you or make your life miserable if you're wrong in one point of procedure. Right or wrong, you can still be in trouble if you don't carry yourself and represent yourself (or your employer) in the right way.

17. Say what you want as long as you do what I say. Needless to say, this is a major street principle for the police. I teach that they should allow a citizen to say what he wants as long as he cooperates. Who cares what he says? He's usually just trying to save face. Remember this when dealing with your children. Unless they're so disrespectful that that in itself is cause for discipline, let them grumble about what you've told them—as long as they comply. Being able to gripe a little gives them the feeling that they still have some say about what happens in their life, even though in reality you are holding the reins.

The only time this is not advisable is when your target audience is on the verge of being out of control and his own words can trigger an adrenaline rush in him or in bystanders that will prove dangerous. The same is true at home. Let your children say what they want as long as they aren't getting a sibling or your spouse agitated at the same time. When that happens you need to address not just their actions but also their words, draw a very clean line, and move to discipline. In other words, before things get out of hand, you might have to say, "You, be quiet. You, go to your room now and I'll be in to see you in a minute. You, put that down and wait here for me."

18. You can have the last word, because I have the last act is a principle associated with the previous one. Obviously it is a police principle and does not apply

when you're simply trying to negotiate with a service person or an equal. But if you're a parent or a boss it applies. You don't want to flaunt it or say it, but knowing it will give you great confidence. Your employee can cuss you out and flip over your desk, and if it fits your purpose you can sit there smiling benignly. He knows as well as you do that the final verdict—likely his dismissal—lies with you.

19. Never use those words that rise most readily to your lips, for the moment you do you will give the greatest speech you'll ever live to regret. This is one I've personally proven more times than I care to remember. I'm an expert at Verbal Karate, lashing out at people, angering them, burning bridges. Never once has it resulted in anything positive. I say my peace and feel great temporarily (see number 21), and then I spend months or years dealing with the fallout of a broken relationship.

    The words that rise most readily to your lips are always reactive rather than responsive. You must choose your words with an eye on the goal: What is the one thing I want to accomplish?

20. If it doesn't work with Mama, don't use it on the street. This is merely a simple way to remember that you have to treat everyone as you treat your family. If it doesn't work to tell your spouse or your kids, "Calm down!" then don't try it with the public.

21. If it makes you feel good, no good. If you say the thing that makes *you* feel the best, nine times out of ten you're making a mistake. Sadly, it makes you feel good to stroke your own ego, to put somebody down, to tear into someone. The only exceptions to this principle are when what makes you feel good is something you know will also make the other person feel good, or when you're using strip phrases as deflectors (" 'preciate that, understan' that, oyesss").

22. Never step on someone's personal face. Allow most everyone to save face. Remember, you have the last

act, so there's no need to put people down. I wish somebody had told me that when I was a teenager, because for many years I made a habit out of doing just that, and it resulted in nothing but broken relationships. You can get into a person's space, but never in his face.

If as a police officer I told somebody, "Hey, you! Come here!" he'd immediately back up. To a person in trouble, "come here" means "go away." What I had to do was to go to him in a nonthreatening manner. When I got in close proximity I'd say, "Excuse me, sir, may I chat with you?"

By then I might have been only about a foot and a half from him, but because I was nonthreatening, I was not in his face.

23. The less ego you show, the more power you have over others. It takes a healthy ego to be a leader, a mover and shaker. I admit I have a good deal of confidence in myself and my ability to communicate, speak, and teach. But if I got up in front of an audience and bragged about that, I would lose them. Put your ego into your job, into the people you supervise, into your goals. But don't show your ego by revealing your personal face in verbal encounters.

The most common complaint about supervisors is that they have their heads in the air, their noses turned up, "they think they're better than us." That's exactly how not to create a cohesive team. Great teams are built by leaders who channel their egos into their people.

The best supervisor will come to work every day to make his people better than he ever was. That was a goal of the ancient masters, to see their students go beyond them. Success comes from others. Put your power into others, let them carry the day, and you will be seen as a successful leader.

24. Men are like steel; when they lose their temper, they are useless. Fine tempered steel has strength. Steel

that lacks temper breaks under stress. This is another principle that goes back to the samurai.

25. When your mouth opens, your ears slam shut. Too many people think leadership has to do with talking. But great leadership has more to do with listening. When you're talking, you cannot listen. Listening is a highly active, artificial skill.

26. Common sense is most uncommon under pressure. Everybody from customers to clients to people on the street know that if they can get under your skin, they're going to own you. Keep your cool and you'll maintain your common sense.

Remember, Verbal Judo is a way, the gentle way, to engage in tactical communication, or what I call contact professionalism. Think of it as a way of life. It is not just for sales, not just to make money, not just to dominate people. It is a way to live with dignity and power and assertiveness. Power is knowledge in action, and the knowledge I hope you've gained from this book has been tested on the street by the finest communicators in America, those whose lives depend on it. Make Verbal Judo part of who you are.